UNIVERSITY OF NORTH CAROLINA AT CHAPEL HILL
DEPARTMENT OF ROMANCE LANGUAGES

NORTH CAROLINA STUDIES
IN THE ROMANCE LANGUAGES AND LITERATURES

Founder: URBAN TIGNER HOLMES
Editor: MARÍA A. SALGADO

Distributed by:

UNIVERSITY OF NORTH CAROLINA PRESS

CHAPEL HILL
North Carolina 27515-2288
U.S.A.

NORTH CAROLINA STUDIES IN THE
ROMANCE LANGUAGES AND LITERATURES
Number 249

CALISTO'S DREAM AND THE CELESTINESQUE
TRADITION: A REREADING OF *CELESTINA*

CALISTO'S DREAM
AND THE
CELESTINESQUE TRADITION:
A REREADING OF *CELESTINA*

BY
RICARDO CASTELLS

CHAPEL HILL

NORTH CAROLINA STUDIES IN THE ROMANCE
LANGUAGES AND LITERATURES
U.N.C. DEPARTMENT OF ROMANCE LANGUAGES

1995

Library of Congress Cataloging-in-Publication Data

Castells, Ricardo, 1954-
 Calisto's dream and the Celestinesque tradition: a rereading of Celestina / by Ricardo Castells.

 138 p. – cm. – (North Carolina Studies in the Romance Languages and Literatures: no. 249)

 Based on the author's doctoral dissertation, Duke University, 1991.
 Includes bibliographical references.
 ISBN 0-8078-9253-X (alk. paper)

 1. Rojas, Fernando de, d. 1541. Celestina. 2. Space and time in literature. 3. Dreams in literature. I. Title. II. Series.
 PQ6428.C289 1995
 862'.2 – dc20

95-8444
CIP

© 1995. Department of Romance Languages. The University of North Carolina at Chapel Hill.

ISBN 0-8078-9253-X

DEPÓSITO LEGAL: V. 1.838 - 1995   I.S.B.N. 84-401-2145-8

ARTES GRÁFICAS SOLER, S. A. - LA OLIVERETA, 28 - 46018 VALENCIA - 1995

CONTENTS

	Page
ACKNOWLEDGEMENTS	13
I. CALISTO'S DREAM AND THE CELESTINESQUE TRADITION	15
II. THE SPATIAL AND THEMATIC UNITY OF *CELESTINA*, ACT I	35
III. TEMPORAL UNITY AND OBJECTIVE TIME IN *CELESTINA*	55
IV. CALISTO AND THE IMPUTED PARODY OF COURTLY LOVE IN *CELESTINA*	79
V. MELIBEA'S SWIFT SURRENDER: CHARACTERIZATION AND SELF-REALIZATION IN *CELESTINA*	99
VI. TOWARDS A NEW VISION OF *CELESTINA*	119
APPENDIX I	131
BIBLIOGRAPHY	135

Para mi familia

"¿El sueño que vas rumiando,
vuelve a ti como a su centro?"

JUAN RAMÓN JIMÉNEZ
Romances de Coral Gables

"Y vas hacia tu centro. Transmutado. A su imagen."

AMANDO FERNÁNDEZ, *Espacio mayor*

"Los enamorados son desta materia: que la imagen de su amiga tienen siempre figurada y fija dentro de sus pensamientos, por donde no pueden ocupar jamás la imaginación en otra cosa; en esta imagen… están trasportados y rebatados todas las horas; con ella hablan, della cantan y della lloran, con ella comen y duermen y despiertan…"

FRANCISCO LÓPEZ DE VILLALOBOS (1544)

ACKNOWLEDGEMENTS

This study, which in its original form was my 1991 doctoral disseration on *Celestina,* was completed with the constant support and assistance of the faculty of the Department of Romance Studies at Duke University. Dr. Bruce W. Wardropper, my thesis director, suggested that I research the relationship between *Celestina* and its progeny, which provided the focus that made this study possible. He supervised the entire work with admirable skill and patience, carefully pointing out problems and omissions, but always with encouragement and understanding.

Dr. Miguel Garci-Gómez suggested the idea of Calisto's vision during a graduate seminar on *Celestina* at Duke, and he was most generous with his ideas on Rojas's work. Dr. Garci-Gómez's concept of *Celestina*'s opening scene represents the core of this study, but just as important is his belief that a proper understanding of the text requires a direct challenge to many of the myths that have marred modern *Celestina* scholarship for decades.

Dr. Gustavo Pérez-Firmat was particularly helpful with his interpretation of act one of *Celestina,* and his ideas form the basis of much of chapter two of this study. Dr. Rafael Osuna's reading of Calisto's role in act one has also been important in my analysis of the protagonist in chapter four. I would like to thank Dr. Philip Stewart for his generous assistance with the thesis, as well as with numerous administrative matters in the department and the Graduate School.

Most importantly, I must thank my family for their infinite patience, support, and good humor throughout this process: my wife Diana; my daughters Carolina, Carmen, and Victoria María; and my parents Rodolfo and Matilde. They have put up with countless evenings at the computer terminal, innumerable weekends at the library, and endless conversations about Calisto and Melibea. To them this work is lovingly dedicated.

MIAMI, FLORIDA
June, 1993

I

CALISTO'S DREAM AND THE CELESTINESQUE TRADITION

Almost five hundred years after the earliest known edition of Fernando de Rojas's *Comedia de Calisto y Melibea,* published in Burgos in 1499, Spanish Renaissance scholars are still debating the many contradictions and uncertainties surrounding the work's opening scene. This brief episode consists of an ambiguous and enigmatic dialogue between Calisto and Melibea, the work's two young protagonists, who soon afterwards begin a secret yet short-lived love affair. The conversation between the two future lovers, which takes place in an unspecified location identified only as a "tan conveniente lugar" (I, 86), is particularly difficult to understand because it is full of unusual and possibly heretical language and imagery. To add to the scene's complexity, the discussion ends with a sudden and inexplicable transformation in Melibea, a change that appears to destroy the continuity between the opening scene and the rest of the first act.

The entire first act of *Celestina* is taken from an anonymous manuscript that Fernando de Rojas apparently found while a student at Salamanca, and which inspired him to write the complete *Comedia* and *Tragicomedia de Calisto y Melibea.* Nevertheless, the unknown *antiguo auctor's* first act – generally known as the *Auto –* does not appear to provide an adequate temporal and spatial framework for the opening scene, so much of our understanding of the episode has been shaped by later additions to the *Celestina* text. Virtually all modern critics believe that the opening scene is correctly described by the *argumento* to the first act of *Celestina,* which explains that, "Entrando Calisto una huerta empos dun falcon suyo, halló ý a Melibea, de cuyo amor preso, començóle de hablar;

de la qual rigorosamente despedido, fue para su casa muy sangustiado" (I, 85).

In the prologue to the *Tragicomedia,* Rojas reveals that the arguments to the original *Comedia* of 1499 were the work of the book's printers, referring to the Burgos workshop of Fadrique Alemán de Basilea. While Rojas acknowledges the arguments' plausibility, he indicates that these summaries represent only one of the many readings of *Celestina* that have appeared as its first readers struggle to understand and interpret the work:

> Assí que quando diez personas se juntaren a oír esta comedia en quien quepa esta differencia de condiciones, como suele acaescer, ¿quién negará que aya contienda en cosa que de tantas maneras se entienda? Que aun los impressores han dado sus punturas, poniendo rúbricas o sumarios al principio de cada auto, narrando en breve lo que dentro contenía; una cosa bien escusada según lo que los antiguos escriptores usaron. (80-81)

While Rojas neither accepts nor rejects the interpretation of the work found in the printers' arguments, modern scholars have demonstrated that these summaries contain numerous deficiencies. According to Marcel Bataillon (1967), "Or cet *argumento [del primer auto],* que vaut-il? Est-ce un résumé assez fidèle de l'acte I pour que nous devions croire que son début résume la scène I? On a au contraire ... dénoncé la maladresse et l'inexactitude des *argumentos* placés en tête des actes" (11). Stephen Gilman (1956) also writes that, "[I]f we as readers want to find out what *La Celestina* is really about, these *argumentos* are the last place to which we ought to turn" (213).

Although Gilman emphasizes the poor quality of the *Comedia*'s original arguments, he curiously excludes the first summary from this critical judgment: "Unlike the first act, the quality of these argumentos – their performance of their descriptive function – is so inadequate that Rojas' disclaimer [in the prologue to the *Tragicomedia*] has generally been believed" (212). Gilman's analysis begs the question of why modern readers would admit *Celestina*'s first argument if all the other arguments do not properly describe the work. It appears that modern scholars may have accepted this first argument because they have not found a better alternative interpretation of the first act, and certainly not because the printers' summary is entirely convincing or free from defects.

Martín de Riquer (1957) is among the first readers to reject the traditional interpretation of the first scene. Riquer reads the primitive text without the arguments because of the difficulty of analyzing a work by two different authors that is bounded by summaries from yet a third writer. He therefore studies act one as closely to its original form as possible to see how the *antiguo auctor*'s work differs from the complete *Celestina* text. Based on this reading, Riquer concludes that the first argument is flawed and that it does not agree with the original intent of the primitive author:

> Si... leemos [la escena] con cuidado y sin prejuicios, observaremos que las primeras palabras que se cruzan los dos jóvenes no revelan en modo alguno un encuentro casual, ya que Calisto afirma que ha hecho una serie de promesas... para conseguir de Dios que le otorgara el galardón de «este lugar alcançar».... Calisto, pese a la afirmación del argumento del acto primero, no parece que haya llegado a presencia de Melibea en pos de un halcón. En toda la escena el ave de caza no se menciona para nada, el joven no hace ni el más pequeño gesto que indique que va en su busca ni que la recoja y la doncella no alude ni tan solo vagamente a un incidente de esta suerte. (384)

Riquer believes that, in its original form in the *antiguo auctor*'s primitive text, the first episode "no transcurría en el huerto de Melibea y no tenía nada que ver con la búsqueda de un halcón" (385). The falcon does not appear in *Celestina* until the conversation between Calisto and Pármeno in Rojas's second act, and Riquer concludes that this version of the meeting has no relation to the episode in the *Auto*.[1] Moreover, since Calisto tells Melibea about his "secreto dolor" and "el servicio, sacrificio, devoción y obras pías que por esté lugar alcançar yo tengo a Dios offrecido" (I, 86), the opening scene cannot be the first encounter between the two future lovers. Riquer proposes a church as the meeting place for Calisto and Melibea because the scene's religious allusions could have been inspired by the church's spiritual atmosphere.

A. Rumeau (1966) agrees that the *Auto*'s first scene is neither the meeting that Pármeno mentions in the the second act, nor the

---

[1] "Señor, porque perderse el otro día el neblí fue causa de tu entrada en la huerta de Melibea a le buscar, la entrada causa de la veer y hablar; la habla engendró amor; el amor parió tu pena; la pena causará perder tu cuerpo y *el* alma y hazienda" (II, 134-35).

same situation described by the printers' first argument. According to Rumeau's reading of the primitive text, the first act begins when an already enamored Calisto declares his love for Melibea inside or near a church. When Pármeno mentions Calisto's encounter with the young woman "el otro día" (II, 134), the servant is referring to the two lovers' first meeting several days before their conversation in scene one. Significantly, Rumeau also observes that neither Calisto nor Melibea ever appear to refer to the conversation in scene one throughout Rojas's continuation of *Celestina*.[2]

W. D. Truesdell (1973) also reads the first act of *Celestina* without the printers' arguments, and concludes that some of Riquer's conclusions are valid and deserving of critical attention. According to Truesdell, "[W]hat was convincing about the Riquer arguments was not the placement of the scene within a church, but rather the proofs that it could not possibly have been in Melibea's garden" (264). The most important element in the opening scene is the lack of any specific location for the dialogue between Calisto and Melibea: "The author could only have been trying to indicate that this initial and all-important scene took place nowhere, outside of conventional space, in unlocalized, 'abstract' space [without spatial and/or temporal concretization]" (265).

Truesdell also emphasizes the religious and undefined nature of Calisto's words: "[Calisto] asks the rhetorical question: 'Quién vido en esta vida cuerpo glorificado de ningún hombre, como agora el mío?'. The phrase 'cuerpo glorificado' is very telling. According to Catholic theology the saints enjoying beatific vision do so without the benefit of their earthly bodies" (268). Since the opening scene is not situated in space and time, Truesdell concludes that the conversation occurs "nowhere, outside of conventional space, in unlocalized, 'abstract' space. One must ask why the primitive author went to such pains to avoid the localization of Scene I, why he strove to create abstraction and universalization for the introduction of his work" (275).

Despite the research by Riquer, Rumeau, and Truesdell, almost all modern scholars still accept the traditional interpretation of the first scene, as evidenced by the work of María Rosa Lida de Malkiel

---

[2] Marcel Bataillon writes that, "Or l'identification de la scène I avec cette première recontre imprévue a été combattue . . . par [A. Rumea] avec des raisons que je crois sans réplique" (1967: 10).

(1962), R. E. Barbera (1970), F. M. Weinberg (1971), Charles B. Faulhaber (1977), and Michael Solomon (1989). Nevertheless, critics who accept the orthodox interpretation perhaps ignore or distort the many textual references that suggest that the first encounter between Calisto and Melibea occurs before the opening scene. Pármeno clearly specifies the date of the two lovers' meeting during the first day of *Celestina* when he says that Calisto lost the falcon "el otro día" (II, 134). This same temporal structure is repeated time and again throughout the work, and is reaffirmed during the fourth and final day of the *Comedia* when Melibea tells her father that, "[M]uchos días son passados . . . que penava por mi amor un cavallero que se llamava Calisto . . ." (XX, 333).³

Because the work specifies that Calisto and Melibea meet before the start of the first act, we are faced with two possible interpretations of the opening scene. Either Rojas changed the meaning of the first scene, as Riquer believes, or there is another way of in-

---

³ There are many other references in Rojas's continuation that indicate that the *Auto*'s opening scene takes place before the beginning of the work:

"MELIBEA. Éste (Calisto) es el quel otro día me vido y començó a desvariar conmigo en razones, haziendo mucho del galán. Dirásle, buena vieja, que si pensó que ya era todo suyo y quedava por él el campo, porque holgué más de consentir sus necedades que castigar su yerro, quise más dexarle por loco que publicar su [grande] atrevimiento" (V, 162-163).

"CALISTO. En sueños la veo tantas noches, que temo no me acontezca como a Alcibíades . . ." (VI, 186).

"MELIBEA. Muchos y muchos días son passados que esse noble cavallero me habló en amor; tanto me fue entonces su habla enojosa quanto después que tú me lo tornaste a nombrar, alegre" (X, 245).

"LUCRECIA. *Señora, mucho antes de agora tengo sentida tu llaga y callado tu desseo; hame fuertemente dolido tu perdición. Quanto tú más me querías encobrir y celar el fuego que te quemava, tanto más sus llamas se manifestavan . . .*" (X, 247). Rojas reiterates in the interpolations to the *Tragicomedia* that the first meeting between Calisto and Melibea took place before the beginning of the work.

"CALISTO. ¡O quántos días antes de agora passados me fue venido esse pensamiento a mi corçón [sic], y por impossible le rechaçava de mi memoria..." (XII, 261).

"MELIBEA. . . . y aunque muchos días he pugnado por lo dissimular, no he podido tanto que, en tornándome aquella mujer tu dulce nombre a la memoria, no descubriesse mi deseo y viniesse a este lugar . . ." (XII, 262).

"CALISTO. Muy cierto es que la tristeza acarrea pensamiento y el mucho pensar impide el sueño, como a mí estos días es acaecido con la desconfiança que tenía de la mayor gloria que ya poseo" (XIII, 276).

terpreting the scene that modern critics may not have grasped. Gilman (1956), Lida de Malkiel (1962), and Severin (1970) affirm *Celestina*'s structural unity, but propose an abstract or subjective time to explain the book's temporal contradictions. For other orthodox critics, the temporal and thematic contradictions between the first act and Rojas's text are the result of the change of author following the first act. Faulhaber (1977), for example, writes that

> We have . . . to reconcile two sets of facts: Act I . . . presuppose[s] that Calisto is in love with Melibea before he speaks to her in the garden. The references in Acts II and IV, and the *argumentos*, imply that the hawk entered the garden by chance, that Calisto followed it, and that he fell in love with Melibea at first sight. In short, Act I is at variance with the argumentos and the rest of the work. This discrepancy confirms the authorial difference between Act I and the other acts, but it also testifies to Rojas' respect for the textual integrity of Act I. (446)

Although it is important to study the change in authors after the first act of *Celestina,* this interpretation ignores the simple but fundamental question of why an author of Rojas's ability would disrupt the continuity of the work in this fashion. At the same time, the notion of an abstract or subjective time is tantamount to an admission that traditional critics are unable to account for the passage of time in *Celestina.* In essence, by stressing the themes of authorial difference and subjective time, modern scholars have done something unique in the study of Hispanic letters: they have accepted the arguments written by a foreign printer or an unknown apprentice over the text written by Fernando de Rojas.

Despite the many contradictions implicit in the traditional interpretation, heterodox critics have also been unable to resolve the enigma of the first act. These scholars argue that the opening scene is not a casual encounter between Calisto and Melibea, and that the two lovers' first meeting does not occur during the work's first day. Nevertheless, they have not managed to localize or fully explain the problematical opening scene. It would be difficult to accept Riquer's view that *Celestina* opens in a church, and it appears virtually impossible to consider Truesdell's idea that the episode occurs in an abstract and undefined place. In order to change the traditional viewpoint, it would be necessary to demonstrate where, how, and when the opening scene takes place, and to develop and define this idea in a logical and coherent fashion.[4]

Miguel Garci-Gómez (1985) attempts to resolve the contradictions that surround the first act of *Celestina* by following the lead of Riquer and Truesdell and reading the first act independently of the arguments. Garci-Gómez again concludes that Calisto's and Melibea's first conversation takes place before the beginning of the work, particularly in light of the repeated temporal references throughout Rojas's continuation. Garci-Gómez also notices that it is Melibea rather than Calisto who disappears from the first scene, and that the primitive author never indicates that Calisto has left his room during this critical episode. If the opening scene does not occur in Melibea's garden, and if Calisto has not left his bedroom during the first episode, then the logical interpretation is that the entire scene has been a dream or vision by an already enamored Calisto:

> La cámara, está claro, es el único lugar mencionado. Sempronio es el único personaje que acompañaba físicamente a Calisto. ¿Y Melibea? Calisto acababa de dialogar con ella. Pero ni la hemos visto allí, físicamente, ni hemos visto que saliera. Su presencia se desvaneció. Como se desvanecen las apariciones. Calisto, ¿quién lo duda?, había tenido una aparición, una visión, un sueño. (14)

This conclusion is surprising for readers who have been conditioned by the printers' argument to the first act, but the idea of Calisto as a dreamer is repeated time and again in *Celestina,* so this interpretation fits with the character of the young protagonist.[5] At the same time, the scene described by Garci-Gómez has an important model in the beginning of the *Paulus*, a humanistic comedy whose similarity with *Celestina* had already been mentioned by Menéndez

---

[4] Miguel Marciales (1985) recognizes the textual difficulties of the first scene in the primitive text, and at the same time offers another possible explanation for the conversation between Calisto and Melibea. According to Marciales, "todo problema desaparece si originariamente Melibea hubiera sido una mujer casada" (I, 84). Although we accept the possiblity of Marciales's thesis because of the lack of detail about Calisto's and Melibea's relationship in the first act, this paper supports a different point of view that has a close relation with the text and with the traditions of the Spanish dramatic novel.
[5] For general studies of Calisto's dreamlike nature, see Marcel Bataillon (1961), chapter 4, "Calisto l'insensé" (108-134); and María Rosa Lida de Malkiel (1962), chapter XII, "Calisto," especially 347-373.

Pelayo and Lida de Malkiel. According to Garci-Gómez, however, there is not a similarity but rather a clear repetition of the episode in the *Paulus*: "En ambas obras los jóvenes protagonistas se despiertan tras haber gozado de un sueño glorioso e increpan, en tono muy destemplado, a uno de los criados" (17, n. 5).

Garci-Gómez's interpretation suggests that Rojas understood and respected the primitive text, and that there is no temporal contradiction between the first act and the continuation of the book. Nevertheless, if we are to accept the idea of the dream, we must demonstrate that contemporary readers would have understood the scene in this fashion, and that the first argument is no more than a misreading by some careless printers. In fact, although the possibility of Calisto's opening dream may seem unusual to modern scholars, it would not surprise most Renaissance readers because this was a common theme in the literature of the period, as we can see in the *Cárcel de amor*, the poetry of Garcilaso, and even in the comedies of Lope de Rueda.[6]

---

[6] In the beginning of the *Cárcel de amor*, for example, Leriano lacks *las armas* of *Descanso* and *Reposo* to defend himself from the scourge of love, so like Calisto he is unable to rest while he suffers the effects of his overwhelming passion. In Garcilaso's second eclogue, Salicio sees Albanio as he wakes up up from a dream in a situation quite similar to Sempronio's and Calisto's dialogue in the first act of Celestina:

> ALBANIO: ¿Es esto sueño, o ciertamente toco
> la blanca mano? ¡Ah, sueño, estás burlando!
> Yo estábate creyendo como loco . . .
> SALICIO: Albanio, deja el llanto, qu'en oíllo
> me aflijo.
> ALBANIO: ¿Quién presente, 'sta a mi duelo?
> SALICIO: Aquí está quien t'ayudará a sentillo
> (lines 113-115 and 122-124).

Another example of this model is seen in Lope de Rueda's *Comedia llamada Eufemia*. The play begins early in the morning in the protagonist's Leonardo's bedroom, but the young man has not slept well because he is worried about his trip that day to arrange his sister's marriage:

> Larga y en demasiada manera me ha parescido la pasada noche. No sé si fue la ocasión el cuidado con que de madrugar me acosté. Sin duda debe de ser ansí, porque buen rato ha que Eufemia, mi querida hermana, con sus criadas siento hablar; que con el mismo pensamiento se fue a dormir, entendiendo de mí que no me pudo apartar de hacer esta jornada. Veréis que no sé si habrá tampoco hecho [el criado] Melchor lo que anoche le dejé encomendado. ¡Melchor! ¡Ah, Melchor! (47)

His cry for his servant reveals that he has broken his train of dreamlike thought, a pattern that is analyzed in chapter two of this study.

For the importance of dreams in Spanish literature before Rojas, see Harriet Goldberg (1983).

Although the young lover's reverie is found in other Renaissance works, the most direct evidence for Calisto's dream appears in the Celestinesque genre, the Spanish Renaissance and Baroque dialogue novels that use *Celestina* as their model text. An analysis of the sixteenth- and seventeenth-century Celestinesque tradition strongly suggests that these authors understood that *Celestina* begins with the *galán*'s dream about Melibea, and that they repeatedly incorporated this *patrón* into the beginning of their own works. More importantly, this study will examine Fernando de Rojas's continuation of *Celestina*, and will demonstrate that Rojas also understood Calisto's opening dream, and that he consciously repeated the same pattern during the second and third mornings of the *Comedia*.

The first works in the Celestinesque style were the *Thebaida*, *Serafina*, and *Ypólita*, three anonymous Valencian comedies published in 1520 or 1521. The *Comedia Thebaida* was apparently written between 1504 and 1520,[7] but while it follows some of the patterns of *Celestina*, it lacks the tragic and didactic elements found in Rojas's work. In the first act of *Thebaida*, the young protagonist Berintho is awake but suffers while he sees his beloved Cantaflua in his imagination:

> ... pues estoy tal que la imaginación y pensamiento un solo momento no se devierte a extraños actos, ni dexa de contemplar su tan immensa y extremada hermosura.... Y cuando ya algún tanto vacío me siento de la tal imaginación, quedo tan laso, quedo tan fatigado y tan sin acuerdo que hago harto en tornar poco a poco a cobrar aliento de nuevo, para con fuerça reziente tornar a emprender el fuego tan intolerable y tan agente en que por su causa a la contina me estoy quemando, sin que su ravia y llama cruel un solo instante me dexe reposar. (9)

Berintho is in his bedroom with his servants Menedemo, Galterio, Simaco and Aminthas, but the comedy makes clear several times that the protagonist does not leave his bed the entire first day:

> BERINTHO. Bien dize Galterio. Acércate más, Menedemo. Y aun ambos os podéis hincar de rodillas en el estrado que está delante la cama, porque [yo] oiga bien lo que dixéredes. (13)

---

[7] Keith Whinnon, "Introduction" to *La comedia Thebaida,* xv-xvii and xxiii-xxviii.

> BERINTHO. Y tú, Menedemo, pues ya es noche enciende velas y llégame la mesa aquí a la cama, y dame papel y escrivanía, y siguiendo el consejo inspirado por spíritu prophético escriviré de mi espacio entretanto que Franquila viene. (30)

Even though Berintho is awake, he suffers so much because of his love for Cantaflua that he is unable to distinguish between reality and his imagination. Even when he sees things around him, they appear to him as though they occurred in a dream: "Algo parece que se me va acordando, pero semeja al pensamiento haver visto todas estas cosas en sueños. Pero procede, [Menedemo,] y podrá ser que cayese algún tanto en la cuenta" (22).

Franquila, the go-between in the *Comedia Thebaida*, arrives at Berintho's house in the fourth act and remains "a los pies de la cama" (53) watching the young man's dreamlike trance:

> Pero entrando vi que Berintho estava hablando a bozes consigo – y ha dicho tantos desatinos que no lo podriedes pensar –, y porque con mi vista tan inopinada no fuesse de un extremo a otro con el amor que me tiene, y la súbita mudança fuese causa de algún inconveniente desastrado, tove por mejor esperarme un poco que no con mi entrada improvisa poner en condición de salud . . . Que le dexemos, specialmente hasta que acabe de devanear. (53)

Berintho recites *romances amorosos* without realizing that Franquila and the other servants are observing him. It is not until the servants see that Berintho is "ya reposado, y [que] ninguna cosa habla" (65) that they awaken him from his somnolent state.

Berintho is not the only lover in the *Comedia Thebaida* who alternates between dreams, delirium, and reality. Cantaflua appears for the first time in the comedy in bed in a lament similar to Berintho's, and she is also unaware that there are other people in the room observing her. Once her servant Claudia realizes that Franquila has brought Cantaflua a letter from Berintho, she immediately awakens the young girl from her long stupor: "¡O cuitada! ¿Y por qué no lo havías dicho antes [, Franquila]? Y hoviéramosla reçucitado aunque estoviera muerta. Espera, espera, y verás por esperiencia lo que digo. Señora, señora, que stá aquí Franquila y os trae una carta de Berintho, y ha dos horas que espera aquí" (103).

Franquila later returns to Berintho's house with Cantaflua's response to the *galán*'s letter, but Berintho remains in bed in the same languorous trance as before. He awakens to hear Franquila's words, but he still has trouble distinguishing between his imagination and the external reality represented by the other characters: "¿Qué es esto lo que dizes a Menedemo [, Franquila]? Que todo cuanto me has dicho tengo entendido, pero aún pienso que estoy durmiendo" (136). At the end of the conversation between Berintho and Franquila, the young man goes back to sleep because this lassitude appears to be a normal state for a young lover: "Ya es tarde, y yo tengo gana de reposar un rato" (150). Later on, when the two servants Aminthas and Claudia fall in love, they also adopt the same dreamlike lethargy as their two masters (189-90; 193-95).

The young protagonist again appears for the first time in a dream sequence in the *Comedia Serafina,* another anonymous Valencian comedy from 1520 or 1521. In the opening scene, the servants Pinardo, Cratino, Popilia, and Davo talk about their master Evandro's love for the married but still virgin Serafina. Cratino comments that,

> La ymaginación en la cosa siempre suele refrescar las llagas, esto de una parte; y tanbién ver a la clara la voluntad de Serafina an dado causa a que el viejo dolor, cobrando aliento de nuevo, con rezientes fuerças a tornado a lo atormentar de tal manera que toda esta noche ni él adormió ni a mí dexó pegar los ojos. (12)

Evandro's delirium also makes him sing *romances amorosos* that continue until Popilia tells the servants to enter the bedroom to awaken him. The master yells for the servants as they come out of the *sala*, so this scene clearly mimics the action between Calisto and Sempronio in the second act of *Celestina*:

> EVANDRO. Moços, moços, ¿estáys ahí?
> CRATINO. A la puerta de la sala estávamos. ¿Qué mandas, señor?
> EVANDRO. ¡O cómo me abraso en el fuego que veo a la clara proceder de los ojos de Serafina!. . . . ¡O cómo la misma discordia está predominando en mi pecho! ¡O cómo la confusión me aconpaña! (19)

Just like Calisto and Berintho, this somnolent torpor is Evandro's normal state, as Penardo observes in a conversation with Popilia:

"Entretanto que ese ciego de razón y falto de entendimiento está devaneando como suele, anda acá a tu cámera . . ." (26).

The *Comedia Ypólita* differs from the other two Valencian comedies because it is written in verse form rather than in prose, and also because it has a male servant fulfilling the role of the go-between. Nevertheless, the protagonist Ypólito shows the same sleeplike trance as Berintho and Evandro. In the work's first scene, Ypólito tells his servants Solento and Jacinto about his beloved Florinda, but he suddenly loses consciousness in the middle of the conversation:

> YPÓLITO. . . . que al sentido y avn all alma
> tanto las fuerças destruye
> que la vida de mí huye
> y el cuerpo también se pasma,
> de ya vencido.
> SOLENTO. ¡O cómo se a amortecido;
> o cómo en todo desmaya!
> JACINTO. ¿Qué nos pena que se vaya?
> Dexátelo assí caído . . . (24-25)

Although the servants comment that Ypólito is "tan decaýdo / y sin alma y sin concierto" (26), he still continues to talk about Florinda during his brief trance. Ypólito wakes up a short while later, but although he is conscious that he has been in a trance dreaming about Florinda, he has no idea whether his servants were at his side listening to his *devaneos:* "¡O Solento, buen amigo! ¿y as me visto penando?" (27).

Although the Valencian comedies have much in common with *Celestina,* the true Celestinesque genre begins with Feliciano de Silva's *Segunda Celestina* (1534). The *Segunda Celestina* narrates the love of the young protagonists Felides and Polandria, but once again with Celestina as the go-between. In Silva's rewriting of Celestina's story, the procuress faked her death in Rojas's work in order to escape from the authorities and to gain revenge on Pármeno and Sempronio. The *Segunda Celestina*'s first scene begins with the suffering of the young protagonist, but this time he is awake and even shows a certain sense of humor about his situation. Felides calls in his two servants, Sigeril and Pandulfo, but it is not immediately clear to the modern reader where the scene takes place. Nevertheless, the closing conversation of the first act reveals that Felides has spent the entire act in his bedroom, as though the author expected the contemporary reader to understand the location from the very beginning of the work:

> SIGERIL. . . . . Y, en tanto, reposa tú, señor, que no has dormido esta noche, y yo iré a dar priessa a este panfarrón [de Pandulfo], no se vaya todo en fieros y palabras su hecho.
> FELIDES. Ansí lo haz; y ve con Dios, y ciérrame esta puerta. (123)

Gaspar Gomez's *Tercera parte de la Tragicomedia de Celestina* (1536) is a continuation of Feliciano de Silva's *Segunda Celestina*, and the first act takes place the morning after the end of the *Segunda Celestina*. Felides and Polandria have spent the evening together and have agreed to marry, but they still need Polandria's father's permission to celebrate a public wedding. In the *Tercera Celestina*, Felides appears in the opening act as he awakens from "el sueño, tan suave para mi contemplación y tanto descanso para mi atribulado coraçón" that he has spent the night with Polandria in her garden (78). Here the idea of the protagonist's opening dream appears to be such a normal part of the Celestinesque genre that Felides thinks that he has dreamed what has occurred in reality:

> Es vn sueño que, avnque es increýble, me causa tanta delectación que affirmo las ymaginaciones que Ouidio escriue de Teseo con Adriena no le diessen la tercia parte désta que tengo. . . . ¡O cómo soy insensato, pues con el deleyte de mi sueño comparo otro ninguno que por la misma forma acontesciesse! (78, 79).

Once again the opening scene takes place in the protagonist's bedroom, with Felides in his bed *devaneando* while his servant waits outside of the bedroom:

> FELIDES. Sigeril, ¿estáys aý?
> SIGERIL. Ansí te puedes secar que yo entre en esta hora, que primero quiero, avnque me duela la cabeça de oýrte, escuchar tus deuaneos. (80)

Despite the obvious resemblance to the opening scene of other Celestinesque texts, the *Tercera Celestina* – as a direct continuation of a previous text – is the only instance where the protagonist begins the book with a dream about an encounter that actually takes place. Gómez uses the opening act of *Celestina* as the model for the beginning for his own work, but he also draws from Calisto's dream in act thirteen of Rojas's novel. Calisto speaks with Melibea in act twelve of *Celestina,* and as he awakens the following morning he suffers the same doubts as Felides about what took place the night before: "O dichoso y bienandante Calisto, si verdad es que no ha sido sueño lo pasado. ¿Soñélo o no? ¿Fue fantaseado o passó en verdad?" (III, 276). Gómez follows the pattern of the opening dream sequence, but he is creative enough to also use another episode that is far more appropriate for the continuation of a love affair.

While *Celestina* creates certain parameters for subsequent authors to follow, these authors use the model text with great flexibility. In later Celestinesque works, the protagonist does not appear in his bed at the beginning of the book, but he soon adopts the same dreamy torpor as the previous protagonists. Bachiller Sebastián Fernández's *Tragedia Policiana* (1547) presents the story of Claudina, Pármeno's mother and Celestina's *comadre.* In the first act, the protagonist Policiano is awake when he calls his servants, but in the third act – when the servants return home after a night of celebration – we see the same somnolent trance that the other Celestinesque protagonists suffer:

> SOLINO. ¿Qué haze nuestro amo? ¿Ha pedido de vestir?
> SILVANICO. Aý está en esta cama que no haze más ruydo que vn muerto. . . . Casa es de locos ésta por la fe en que creo. El amo troba, los moços van a rondar, pues algún día no ha poder que no sea la mía.
> SALUCIO. ¿Troba por auentura el triste de Policiano?
> SILVANICO. Doy al diablo otra cosa haze sino dezir disparates; llora como niño, da bozes como loco, no sé qué tiene.
> POLICIANO. Oyes, paje.
> SILVANICO. Señor.
> POLICIANO. ¿Es de día?
> SILVANICO. E muy gran parte passada.
> POLICIANO. O desdichado de mí, que después que mi coraçón se escuresció, no sé qué cosa es ver claridad. Yo no entiendo quándo amanesce, sino a caso no es por oýdas. (7)

Alonso de Villegas Selvago's *Comedia Selvagia* (1554) is somewhat different from the other Celestinesque novels because it presents two male protagonists, Flerinardo and Selvago. The two young gentlemen discuss the difference between chaste love and dishonest love in the first act, but in the third act Flerinardo awakens from a dream in which he converses with his beloved Rosiana in almost the same way that Calisto speaks with Melibea in *Celestina*'s opening dream:

> No otro sino que habiendo toda la noche gastado en diversos pensamientos, ya cerca de la aurora me vino un profundo sueño, en el qual. . . . la señora que en captividad mi corazón tiene puesto, se me demostró con tanta ira y enojo contra mí, quanta hermosura y beldad para con todos tiene; . . . Habiendo, pues, algún tanto mis muchos miedos considerado, con algo más apacible rostro, desta manera me habló. "¡O tú, que por tan mi verdadero captivo te has mostrado, . . . como a la verdad eres digno a que rigurosamente mi crueldad contra tu locura proceda, pues no solamente violaste mi limpieza con tu dañado pensamiento, mas, aun poniendo mi honra en condición, te jactas y vanaglorias a todos manifestarlo". (57)

Fleriano explains his honest intentions to Rosiana in the dream, and she quickly changes her tone towards the lovesick *galán*:

> Entonces ella, con rostro amoroso y apacible, me respondió en esta manera: "Por ver tu mucha contrición, y que aun el pecado no se puso por obra, yo quiero por ahora perdonarte . . ." Pues dichas estas palabras, súbitamente de mi vista se desapareció, y yo de aquel profundo sueño fui libre. (58-59)

It is important to note that Rosiana repeats Melibea's sudden change of character in the first act of *Celestina*, but in precisely the opposite direction. Rosiana abruptly turns from fury to tranquility in order to praise the honest love that is the principal theme of the *Comedia Selvagia*. Despite this difference, the influence of *Celestina*'s opening scene is quite strong. Alonso de Villegas repeats the dreamworld conversation between the lovers, the anguished young man who clings to his beloved's every word, the sudden disappearance of the young woman, and the protagonist who awakens from the dream once the vision of his *amada* disappears.

This is not the only time in the work that a protagonist is pictured in a dreamworld dominated by thoughts of his beloved. The second *galán* Selvago also follows the same pattern the morning after he meets the beautiful Isabel:

> ¡Válame el poderoso Dios! ¿Qué será esto? ¿Por ventura no estaba yo agora en el reino de mi señora, lleno de su gracia y gozando de su soberana gloria? Pues, ¿cómo me hallo en mi lecho? Sin duda que con algún fingido ensueño he sido engañado; bien será me certifique de segunda persona. ¡Mozos, mozos! (134)

Selvago, like the other Celestinesque protagonists, yells for his servants as soon as he awakens, and then begins to play the lute and sing *romances amorosos.*

The final example of the Celestinesque genre is Lope de Vega's dialogue novel *La Dorotea,* published in Madrid in 1632. Don Fernando, the protagonist, does not appear in the book until the fourth scene of the first act, but once again we see the young man in his bedroom as he awakens. Following the tradition of previous Celestinesque works, don Fernando is bothered by a dream, as he reveals in his first words to his servant Julio:

> JULIO. Con poca gracia te levantas.
> FERNANDO. Mil desasosiegos he tenido esta noche.
> JULIO. ¿No has dormido?
> FERNANDO. Poco y con mil congojas.
> JULIO. Del calor serían.
> FERNANDO. No, sino del primer sueño.
> JULIO. ¿Qué soñabas?
> FERNANDO. Una confusión de cosas. (90)

Fernando has suffered a nightmare in which Dorotea and her servant Celia disembark from an American ship with their hands full of gold, but as they leave the ship they walk by Fernando without addressing him. The dream alludes to the wealth of the *indiano* don Bela, another of Dorotea's suitors, but Dorotea's rejection of Fernando also mirrors Melibea's rejection of Calisto at the beginning of *Celestina.* Although the two scenes are not identical, there are numerous similarities that demonstrate how well Lope knew *Celestina.* Both protagonists have the same *estado de ánimo* – probably because of a bad dream in both cases – and Fernando soon mimics Calisto and begins to sing *romances amorosos* as he shuts himself off in the darkness of his bedroom: "Muerto soy, Julio. Cierra todas las ventanas, no entre luz a mis ojos, pues se va para siempre la que lo fue para mi alma" (111).

Even though all the Celestinesque works do not have precisely the same beginning, the protagonists repeatedly appear in a dreamlike trance in all of the works cited. At the same time, the idea of the dreamworld becomes so closely associated with the dramatic novel that Pedro Hurtado de Vera uses this form to write his allegorical *Doleria del sueño del mundo* (1572), where the entire work is a dream. Without question, the tremendous similarites in the initial presentation of the *galán enamorado* in no less than eight Celestinesque works – the *Comedia Thebaida*, the *Comedia Serafina*, the *Comedia Ypólita*, the *Segunda Celestina*, the *Tercera Celestina*, the *Tragedia Policiana*, the *Comedia Selvagia*, and *La Dorotea* – strongly suggest that all of them are based on a common interpretation of the first act of *Celestina*.

It appears that the writers who continued the Celestinesque tradition saw Calisto in a dream at the beginning of the *Auto,* and so they continued this tradition for well over a century as they reworked the story for their own ends. And although the similarity in these later works does not permit us to establish the *antiguo auctor*'s or Rojas's precise authorial intent, it does offer strong evidence that many readers in fifteenth- and sixteenth-century Spain understood that *Celestina* began in the bedroom of a languorous and lovesick Calisto. Significantly, the Celestinesque genre completely ignores the orthodox interpretation of the opening scene of *Celestina*. None of these works begins with a chance encounter between the two lovers, nor with a scene in the young woman's garden, either of which would be expected if later authors shared the traditional interpretation of scene one. The protagonists are usually in love when the works begin, and they are either in bed in the first scene or will soon be suffering from a lovesick trance in their chamber.

Although the Celestinesque tradition confirms Garci-Gómez's reading of the opening scene, this interpretation finds even more important support in the way Rojas prepares the two additions to *Celestina*. Rojas begins the continuation of the text by stressing Calisto's dreamlike existence early in act two of the *Comedia*. After

Celestina leaves Calisto's house in act one, Sempronio advises his master to return to bed and to count on everyone else's support in his effort to win over Melibea. Sempronio understands that Calisto is incapable of independent action and that his bed is his natural habitat: "de mi consejo tórnate a la cámara y reposa, pues que tu negocio en tales manos está depositado" (II, 131).

Sempronio tells Calisto that he should not remain alone because, "en viéndote solo, dizes desvaríos de hombre sin seso, sospirando, gemiendo, maltrobando, holgando con lo escuro, desseando soledad, buscando nuevos modos de pensativo tormento" (II, 132). Calisto responds that he cannot leave his imaginary world because it provides the only spiritual comfort to his ever-present torment: "¿Cómo, simple, no sabes que alivia la pena llorar la causa? ¿Quánto es dulce a los tristes quexar su passión? ¿Quánto descanso traen consigo los quebrantados sospiros?" (II, 132). Calisto finally accepts that he should not be alone and that Pármeno should accompany him, but his trance-like state is such that he does not realize that Pármeno is already standing at his side:

> PÁRMENO. Aquí estoy señor.
> CALISTO. Yo no, pues no te veýa. (II, 133)

In the sixth act, Calisto reveals that he dreams about Melibea every evening, and that he is very troubled by these visions: "En sueños la veo tantas noches que temo no me acontezca como a Alcibíades . . . , que . . . soñó que se veýa embuelto en el manto de su amiga y otro día mataronle . . ." (VI, 186). Rojas did not invent the notion of Calisto's dream, but his references to this idea during the *Comedia*'s first day create a conscious link to the primitive text. If Rojas tells us that Calisto dreams about Melibea every night, it is because he understands that act one begins in precisely this fashion.

In the eighth act, Pármeno return home after spending the night with Areúsa, and once again Calisto is in bed dreaming about Melibea, the same thing he did the morning before in the opening scene of act one. This episode is a mirror image of the first act because Calisto is playing the lute and "devaneando entre sueños" in his bedroom (VIII, 218). He soon calls the *mozos* in from the hall to attend to him, again like the first act. As the work develops, Calisto enters more and more into this dreamworld. He dissociates himself from external reality and lives exclusively for this love, whether at night in Melibea's garden or during the day in the languorous paradise of his bedroom.

After Sempronio's and Pármeno's death in act twelve, Calisto returns to his room and converses with an imaginary judge in act fourteen. This act represents the beginning of the interpolated scenes of the *Tragicomedia,* so once again Rojas begins his continuation of *Celestina* by stressing Calisto's dreamworld. When Calisto realizes that the conversation with the judge is merely a vision – "Pero, ¿qué digo; con quién hablo; estoy en mi seso? ¿Qué es esto, Calisto; soñavas; duermes o velas; estás en pie o acostado? Cata que estás en tu cámara" (XIV, 290) – he does not want to return to his external reality but rather relive his conversations with Melibea:

> Pero tú, dulce ymaginación, tú que puedes me acorre; trae a mi fantasía la presencia angélica de aquella ymagen luziente; buelve a mis oýdos el suave son de sus palabras, aquellos desvíos sin gana, aquel "apártate allá, señor, no llegues a mí", aquel "no seas descortés" que con sus rubicundos labrios vía asonar; aquel "no quieras mi perdición" que de rato en rato proponía; aquellos amorosos abraços entre palabra y palabra. (XIV, 292-93)

Melibea's words fill Calisto's imagination just as in the first scene of *Celestina,* but now in a happy mixture of fantasy and reality that anticipates the beginning of the *Tercera Celestina.*

Rojas completes *Celestina* twice, first in act two of the *Comedia,* and later in the interpolations that start in act fourteen of the *Tragicomedia.* Both times Rojas begins his rewriting of *Celestina* by stressing Calisto's dreamlike nature, which reinforces his presentation of Calisto's opening dreams during the second and third mornings of the *Comedia.* Both elements suggest that he saw Calisto in a dream in the opening scene of the *Auto,* and that he decided to begin his own texts in the same fashion. It is unsurprising that other Celestinesque writers used a similar point of departure for their own works since they repeated Rojas's creative act of rewriting the primitive author's story of Calisto and Melibea.

Garci-Gómez's interpretation of the first act of *Celestina* may seem surprising to modern critics, but this interpretation conforms to Calisto's personality and confirms *Celestina*'s thematic and temporal unity. This idea resolves the apparent contradictions between the primitive text and Rojas's continuation of *Celestina,* and leaves the printers' arguments as the book's only significant discordant element. Most importantly, the dream sequence has a direct link with the Celestinesque literary tradition, which suggests that Calisto's dream was accepted and understood in Renaissance and Baroque Spain.

II

THE SPATIAL AND THEMATIC UNITY OF *CELESTINA*, ACT I

The first of act of *Celestina* has created numerous problems for modern scholars because of the textual difficulties of the primitive author's *Auto* and its apparent inconsistencies with Fernando de Rojas's continuation of the work. Rojas explains the first act's unusual origin in "El autor a un su amigo," which appears in the Toledo edition of 1500. Here Rojas reveals that he found some anonymous papers that he read again and again because of "su primor, su sotil artificio, . . . su estilo elegante, jamás en nuestra castellana lengua visto ni oýdo" (62). He decided to finish the work during a fifteen-day vacation from the University of Salamanca, but he left the primitive text intact as the first act of *La comedia de Calisto y Melibea*. This unique and improbable genesis has led modern critics to debate the identity of the *antiguo auctor*, the location and the significance of the opening scene, the accuracy of Rojas's transcription of the *Auto,* and even whether Rojas is the principal author of the main text.[1]

One thing that virtually all scholars agree upon is that there is a temporal separation between the *Auto*'s first two scenes, although there is significant disagreement about how to account for this discontinuity. The opening scene appears to be a confusing and contradictory dialogue between Calisto and Melibea that ends with the young woman's fury and Calisto's anguished cry of "Yré como aquél contra quien solamente la adversa Fortuna pone su studio con odio cruel" (I, 87). The second scene apparently begins some

---

[1] See for example Riquer (1957), Faulhaber (1977), Marciales (1983), Sánchez-Sánchez Serrano (1989), and Solomon (1989).

time later in Calisto's house when the young master shouts for his servant: "¡Sempronio, Sempronio, Sempronio! ¿Dónde está este maldicto?" (I, 87).

Modern critics have accepted the temporal separation between these two scenes for two fundamental reasons. First of all, the printer's opening argument to the first act indicates that Calisto meets Melibea at the young woman's garden while hawking, and that he returns home dejectedly after her brusque rejection of his advances. Second, Rojas's continuation of *Celestina* repeatedly suggests that the initial meeting between Calisto and Melibea takes place *el otro día* or *muchos días* before, and certainly not during the first day of the book's action.

Rojas includes both dramatic elements in an important comment by Pármeno in act two, which occurs during the book's first morning: "Señor, porque perderse el otro día el neblí fue causa de tu entrada en la huerta de Melibea a le buscar, la entrada causa de la veer y hablar; la habla engendró amor; el amor parió tu pena; la pena causará perder tu cuerpo y *el* alma y hazienda" (II, 134-35). Pármeno's comments represent a simple summary of the entire text, but they also suggest that the explanation for Calisto's and Melibea's initial meeting should also be simple and readily comprehensible. Nevertheless, while we know that the two future lovers meet several days before the beginning of scene two, modern scholars have lacked a coherent temporal and spatial definition for the book's opening scene. This apparent contradiction has led many critics to debate how to conceptualize and properly account for the articulation of *Celestina*'s first two scenes.

Stephen Gilman (1945, 1953, 1956) attempts to resolve the temporal contradictions in *Celestina* by affirming that there are two different forms of time in the book. There is the objective or external time evidenced by the passing of the hours and the days, along with the characters' internal or subjective time that progresses at a totally different rate from the external time. This subjective time allows the characters to compress and expand events within the *Comedia*'s limited external time frame, and explains why the first meeting between the two lovers can take place days before the rest of the action and still fit within the book's temporal structure.

Manuel Asensio (1952, 1953) disagrees with Gilman's analysis, and states that there is only one basic, objective time throughout *Celestina*. According to Asensio, the opening scene is a prologue to the action, which accounts for the references to Calisto's and Melibea's meeting that occurs several days before the first day of the work. María Rosa Lida de Malkiel (1962) disagrees with Asensio and writes that *Celestina* has an unrealistic temporal development that would explain the separation between the first two scenes. Dorothy Sherman Severin (1970) also believes that the temporal contradictions in the beginning of the book can be explained by the characters' subjective viewpoint towards the passing of time.

More recently, James R. Stamm (1988) studies the seemingly different time frames in the original *Auto* and in Rojas's complete *Celestina*. Stamm accepts Asensio's idea that scene one is the book's prologue, but he concludes that there is only a brief separation between the *Auto*'s first two scenes: "Es difícil suponer que haya pasado más que el breve tiempo necesario para cruzar la distancia que mide entre el 'lugar oportuno' del encuentro con Melibea y los umbrales de [la] casa [de Calisto]" (39-40). While there is only a small temporal division in the original *Auto*, Stamm believes that Rojas changes the form of the first act in his continuation of *Celestina* by creating a longer separation between the work's first two scenes:

> La *Comedia* se aparta radicalmente del sentido del *Auto* en la separación temporal del Prólogo Dramático de la acción que comienza con la segunda escena. Repetidas veces . . . Rojas coloca el primer encuentro de los futuros amantes en un pasado indefinido, pero claramente separado de la acción que ocurre en los cuatro días de la *Comedia*. (146-47)

As we have noted in chapter one of this study, Miguel Garci-Gómez presents a new interpretation of *Celestina*'s opening scene when he concludes that the work begins when an already enamored Calisto suffers an unpleasant dream or vision about his beloved Melibea. We have also demonstrated that the idea of the protagonist's opening dream is a commonplace in the Celestinesque genre for more than a century. Nevertheless, despite the evidence that *Celestina* begins with Calisto's dream, we are still faced with the problem of the articulation of the book's first two scenes. To fully confirm the idea of the opening dream or vision, we would require strong textual evidence to link these two scenes in space and time because the idea of the dream does not permit an interval between the two episodes. We must therefore demonstrate that there is a definite connection between Calisto's, "Yré como aquél contra quien solamente la adversa Fortuna pone su studio con odio cruel," and the apparently unrelated, "¡Sempronio, Sempronio, Sempronio! ¿Dónde está este maldicto?" (I, 87).

A reading of the Celestinesque genre reveals that this evidence indeed exists because many of the male protagonists in these dialogue novels awaken from their lovesick dreams by calling out for their servants. We will use the Celestinesque works and Rojas's continuation of the text to show that Calisto's cry for Sempronio in scene two of *Celestina* does not represent a new location for the action, and that it instead confirms that Calisto has just awakened from a dream about Melibea in his bedroom. This study will establish the temporal and spatial connection between *Celestina*'s first two scenes by examining similar episodes in the *Comedia Serafina*, the *Segunda Celestina*, the *Tercera Celestina*, the *Tragedia Policiana*, the *Comedia Selvagia*, as well as Lope de Rueda's *Comedia llamada Eufemia*.

In the anonymous *Comedia Serafina*, the protagonist Evandro sings *romances amorosos* in his chamber at the beginning of the work while his servants wait outside and discuss his sorrowful condition. Cratino comments that Evandro's love for Serafina has "con rezientes fuerças a tornado a lo atormentar de tal manera que toda esta noche ni él adormió ni a mí dexó pegar los ojos" (13). Evandro begins the second act by interrupting his *romances* and calling for the servants: "Moços, moços, ¿estáys ahí?" (19). In the *Comedia Serafina*, as in the other works we will examine, Evandro's cry for his servants is an indication that he has stopped his *devaneos,* and also serves as the bridge that links the opening episode with the rest of the work.

Feliciano de Silva's *Segunda Celestina* begins with a monologue by the protagonist Felides. The young man laments his unrequited love for Polandria, and decides that he needs the assistance of his faithful servant Sigeril in this endeavor:

> ... en el consejo que tú [el amor] niegas en mi mal quiero pedir a mi sabio y fiel criado Sigeril, podrá ser que como libre de ti, pueda mejor dar consejo en el que a mí me falta. Por tanto quiérole llamar. ¡Sigeril, Sigeril! (114)

Gaspar Gómez's *Tercera Celestina* is a direct continuation of Silva's *Segunda Celestina*. Felides spends the evening with Polandria in her garden at the end of the *Segunda Celestina,* and the continuation begins in the protagonist's bedroom as he dreams about their evening together. Once again Felides interrupts his musings by calling for his servant, who has been outside of his door listening to his master's *devaneos*:

> FELIDES. ¡O cómo soy insensato, pues con el deleyte de mi sueño comparo otro ninguno que por la misma forma acontesciesse! ... Ora tarde se me haze, según la claridad en esta recámara entra. Quiero llamar a Sigeril y darle parte de mis reuelaciones, porque sé que holgará de oýrlo. ... Sigeril, ¿estáys aý?
>
> SIGERIL. Ansí te puedes secar que yo entre en esta hora, que primero quiero, avnque me duela la cabeça de oýrte, escuchar tus deuaneos. (79-80)

At the beginning of Bachiller Sebastián Fernández's *Tragedia Policiana,* the protagonist Policiano is outside his bedroom, thinking about his beloved Philomena:

> Después que mis ojos temerariamente miraron aquella diana figura, ante quien no eran dignos de parescer, ay de mí, que siento en lo secreto de mis entrañas continua guerra, el rostro de ninguna paz. ... Pues bienaventurada passión que tan alto tiene el objecto. Moços, moços. (2-3)

Policiano's call for his servants is not the only common point between the *Tragedia Policiana* and the beginning of *Celestina.* Policiano tells his servant Solino that he fell in love with Philomena when he saw her a few days earlier in a *huerta* – again, some time before the beginning of the story – so the parallel with the *Celestina* model is quite evident:

> ... has de saber, mi Solino, que ha pocos días que passando yo a la huerta de los cipresses por mirar la ribera que muy apazible estava ... vi acompañada de ciertas donzellas una que que a mi parescer privava al Sol de su resplandor phebeo. ... (3)

The *Tragedia Policiana,* like *Celestina,* repeats the device of the master calling for the servants from his bedroom during the book's second day (*Celestina,* VIII, 219). In the third act of the *Tragedia*

Policiana, the servants return home after a night of revelry to find their master in the midst of the typical *devaneos* of the Celestinesque protagonist, but once again Policiano interrupts the dream by yelling for his servants:

> SALUCIO. ¿Troba por auentura el triste de Policiano?
> SILVANICO. Doy al diablo otra cosa haze sino dezir disparates; llora como niño, da bozes como loco, no sé qué tiene.
> POLICIANO. Oyes, paje
> SILVANICO. Señor. (7)

There is another example of the link between the protagonist's dream and his cry for his servants in Alonso de Villegas's *Comedia Selvagia.* Athough this comedy features two protagonists instead of one, the influence of *Celestina*'s opening scene is quite strong in several of the episodes. In scene three of act one, Flerinardo begins the comedy's second day by yelling for his servants from his bedroom:

> FLERINARDO. ¡Mozos, mozos!
> VELMONTE. Señor.
> FLERINARDO. ¿Es de día?
> VELMONTE. Más acertado fuera preguntar si era hora de comer. (52)

Selvago, the second protagonist, soon arrives at the house, and Flerinardo tells him that he has just awakened from a dream about his beloved Rosiana. In the dream, Flerinardo and Rosiana carry on a conversation that is a clear rewriting of the first scene of *Celestina.* While Flerinardo clings to his beloved's every word, Rosiana fluctuates between anger and acceptance, and then suddenly disappears. Flerinardo abruptly awakens from the dream once the vision of his beloved vanishes: "Pues dichas estas palabras, súbitamente de mi vista [Rosiana] se desapareció, y yo del aquel profundo sueño fui libre" (59). Just as in the other cases, the cry for the servant occurs as soon as the young man wakes up from his dream.

Selvago is later pictured in a dreamworld the morning after he meets Isabel, and he too calls for his servants once he awakens from his dream about the young woman:

> ¿Qué será esto? ¿Por ventura no estaba yo agora en el reino de mi señora, lleno de su gracia y gozando de su soberana gloria? Pues, ¿cómo me hallo en mi lecho? Sin duda que con algún fingido ensueño he sido engañado; bien será me certifique de segunda persona. ¡Mozos, mozos! (134)

Selvago, like the other Celestinesque protagonists, then begins to play the lute and sing *romances amorosos* while his servants listen attentively to the music.

There is an additional episode that parallels the first two scenes of *Celestina* in Lope de Rueda's *Comedia llamada Eufemia,* a drama that is outside of the Celestinesque genre. As the play begins, Leonardo cannot sleep because he is thinking about the trip he must make that morning to arrange his sister Eufemia's marriage. The cry for the servant again serves as the bridge between the protagonist's dreamlike thoughts and the continuation of the comedy: "Larga y en demasiada manera me ha parescido la pasada noche. ... Veréis que no sé si habrá tampoco hecho [mi criado] Melchior lo que anoche le dejé encomendado. ¡Melchior! ¡Ah, Melchior!" (47).

It is evident from the works cited that these Renaissance authors used the young master's cry for his servant as the link between the protagonist's dreams and the story's live action. The repeated use of this device suggests that these authors interpreted Calisto's cries for Sempronio in the first act of *Celestina* in the same fashion, and that they understood that there was no temporal or spatial separation between the book's first two scenes. More importantly for modern critics, an examination of *Celestina* indicates that Fernando de Rojas interpreted the *Auto*'s opening scenes in precisely the same way, and that he never intended the first act to be a prologue to the rest of the book.

In the original *Comedia,* Calisto awakens during the second and third mornings by shouting for his servants, just as he does when he awakens in act one. During the second morning, Sempronio tells Pármeno that Calisto "está tendido en el strado cabe la cama donde le dexaste anoche, que ni ha dormido ni está despierto. Si allá entro, ronca; si me salgo, canta o devanea" (VIII, 217). Once Calisto hears the servants outside, he immediately ceases his *devaneos* and calls for them to enter his bedroom: "¿Quién habla en la sala? ¡Moços!" (VIII, 219). The following day, Calisto sleeps soundly because he imagines that Melibea loves him, but he is confused whether their meeting the night before has been a dream or reality. He begins to reason with himself about this problem, but he once again interrupts his thoughts by shouting for his servants:

> O dichoso y bienandante Calisto, si verdad es que no ha sido sueño lo passado. ¿Soñélo o no? ¿Fue fantaseado o passó en verdad? Pues no estuve solo; mis criados me [a]compañaron.... Quiero mandarlos llamar para más confirmar mi gozo. ¡Tristanico, moços, Tristanico, levanta de aý!" (XIII, 276).

During the three mornings that Calisto appears in the *Comedia*, his cries for his servants occur in the precise moment that he stops dreaming or imagining about Melibea, which confirms the thematic unity between the primitive text and the continuation of the work. For Fernando de Rojas, the *Auto* is much more than an intertext with a prologue that he can adapt and modify at will as he creates a new, more complete version of *Celestina*. Rojas has made the first act into an *intratext* that is completely subsumed within the larger *Celestina* text, so he must establish strong and tangible bonds between the *Auto* and his own work. Rojas understands that the primitive author's first act begins *in medias res* with Calisto already lovesick over Melibea, but he has to explain in act two how Calisto got into this predicament without contradicting the action of the *Auto*.

Rojas therefore has to write not only the continuation of *Celestina*, but also the pre-history of Calisto and Melibea because of the *Auto*'s lack of detail about the exact relationship between the two lovers.[2] Since it would be awkward to introduce a complicated

---

[2] Miguel Marciales (1983) has noted the differences between Rojas's *Continuación* and act one, which he calls Rodrigo Cota's *Esbozo:* "Pero la *Continuación* que escribió Rojas no se desprende fatalmente del *Esbozo*, ni mucho menos: sobre aquel *Esbozo* de Cota, sin cambiar un ápice del texto, cabe hacer a Melibea casada con Pleberio y construir una *Fiameta* o una *Historia de los dos amanates*. O hacer a Melibea soltera y/o continuar con una versión de Tristán e Isolda o Pablo y Francisca o de don Melón y doña Endrina" (15).

Miguel Garci-Gómez (1987) also writes about Rojas's interpretation and handling of the primitive text: "¿Que dónde, cómo y cuándo se habían conocido por vez primera Calisto y Melibea? Esa debió ser la pregunta que primero que ningún otro se hiciera Fernando de Rojas al leer aquellos papeles, 'sin firma de su auctor', que parecían comenzar *in medias res*. Preocupado por encontrarle una conveniente respuesta a esa pregunta y lograr con ella una adecuada motivación dramática a la escena, encargó a Pármeno, en el Acto II, el primero de su continuación, la explicación de cómo fue que se encontraron por primera vez Calisto y Melibea" (10).

enredo to an existing story in act two, Rojas limits himself to two key points about the pre-history. First, Calisto has spoken to Melibea only once before when his falcon entered Melibea's garden by chance some days earlier. Second, Calisto believes that another meeting with Melibea is impossible. The contradiction between these two simple facts – both of which are contained in the beginning of the conversation between Calisto and Pármeno in act two (II, 134-35) – establishes Rojas's explanation for the protagonist's desperate condition and fitful dreams in the first scene. More importantly, Rojas uses this explanation to create a logical time frame for the development of the story while he preserves and respects the temporal structure of the first act.[3]

Calisto's shout for Sempronio in the second scene of *Celestina* appears to be an insignificant element in the primitive *Auto*, but our analysis of the Celestinesque tradition reveals that it is an important indication that Calisto has just awakened from a dream about Melibea. As Garci-Gómez has written, Calisto never leaves his room at the beginning of the work, so there is no temporal division between scenes one and two of *Celestina*. The *antiguo auctor*'s first act is a comprehensible, logical narrative, which is precisely why it provides such a solid foundation for Fernando de Rojas's *Celestina*, and also the reason why Rojas successfully conserves and incorporates the primitive *Auto* within his own text.

While Calisto's cry for Sempronio establishes the temporal and spatial connection between the work's first two scenes, there are also important thematic links between the first scene and the rest of the *Auto*. The primitive text exhibits an orderly progression from the immaterial universe of the opening scene to the completely physical and sensual level dominated by Celestina. This progression illustrates what Mikhail Bakhtin (1984) calls the degradation of the medieval canon by Renaissance grotesque realism (21), a change that emphasizes the importance of the physical rather than the intellectual world. Calisto's dreams disappear during the *Auto* as he

---

[3] Numerous scholars have attempted to prove the authorial difference between the *antiguo auctor*'s act one and Rojas's continuation of *Celestina* by pointing out the apparent contradictions between the two texts. While we show that Rojas's work is far more consistent with the *Auto* than previously thought, the way Rojas supplies the story's missing details at the beginning of act two supports the idea of a separate author for the *Auto*. For previous studies on this question, see Riquer (1957); Gilman (1972: 60); and Faulhaber (1977: 446).

becomes engrossed with the carnal nature of his love, so the action descends from elevated mental concepts to lower and more powerful physical compulsions. According to Bakhtin,

> The essential principle of grotesque realism is degradation, that is, the lowering of all that is high, spiritual, ideal, abstract; it is a transfer to the material level, to the sphere of the earth and body in their indissoluble unity.... "Downward" is earth, "upward" is heaven. Earth is an element that devours, swallows up (the grave, the womb) and at the same time an element of birth, of renascence (the maternal breasts). Such is the meaning of "upward" and "downward" in their cosmic aspect, while in their purely bodily aspect, which is not clearly distinct from the cosmic, the upper part is the face or the head and the lower part the genital organs, the belly, and the buttocks. (19-21)

Our analysis of the primitive text suggests that Calisto moves away from the spiritual and abstract sphere of his visions of Melibea, and that he willingly descends into the material and bodily level of physical desires. He will no longer exist in a nebulous mental plane, but rather on Celestina's material level. Calisto's development as a character is closely related to Bakhtin's notion of degradation, which is precisely this descent from mental to physical reality:

> Degradation here means coming back down to earth, the contact with earth as an element that swallows up and gives birth at the same time.... To degrade also means to concern oneself with the lower stratum of the body, the life of the belly and the reproductive organs; it therefore relates to acts of defecation and copulation, conception, pregnancy, and birth.... To degrade an object does not imply merely hurling it into the void of nonexistence, into absolute destruction, but to hurl it down to the reproductive lower stratum, the zone in which conception and a new birth take place. Grotesque realism knows no other lower level; it is the fruitful earth and the womb. It is always conceiving. (21)

The *Auto*'s four main characters can be divided into autonomous, physical characters who live in the material sphere (Celestina and Sempronio), and dependent, theoretical characters who begin the text as idealistic members of an abstract world (Calisto and Pármeno). The two autonomous characters have the spatial facility to move between Calisto's and Celestina's houses, and to converse and scheme both inside and outside the houses. Celestina and Sempronio represent direct contact with and knowledge of the material world, and they enjoy the freedom to speak in frequent asides, to lie to and to cajole the two dependent characters, and to control the development of the story.

Calisto and Pármeno begin the *Auto* as cerebral, idealistic characters with little contact with the outside world. They are symbolically closed off within Calisto's house, but Melibea and Areúsa, the objects of their desire, are distant and unattainable ideals. The two young men lack the initiative and the practical experience to realize their material desires, so they are forced to rely on the mediation of Celestina and Sempronio in order to establish contact with the outside world. Calisto and Párameno are lost within a theoretical plane that must be brought down to an earthly level, but they confirm their dependency on Celestina and Sempronio when they expand and grow to acquire this worldly knowledge.

A fundamental aspect of Bakhtin's decline into grotesque realism is the creative disorder that exists within the physical plane. When Celestina subverts established rules and norms, the text shows a tremendous affirmation of life and of the wonders of the human body. In artistic terms, the primitive text explores a rich, creative vein that affirms its connection with the Renaissance tradition. The *Auto* as a text simply cannot be bound by the traditional canon of medieval courtly love seen in contemporary works such as the *Cárcel de amor*. The primitive text's dynamic realism overwhelms the literary constraints of these earlier texts in its search for more creative artistic expression, in much the same way that Celestina overruns Calisto's and Párameno's immaterial and static world.

Calisto is the first of the two immaterial characters to descend into the material world. The protagonist's degradation is carefully laid out into six distinct steps that reveal the *Auto*'s thematic progression and coherent structure. The first two steps are within the immaterial world, the second two in the descriptive and verbal plane, and the last two in the physical and material sphere. The division between these three groups takes place first when Calisto mentions Melibea (I, 93), and later when Sempronio mentions Celestina (I, 103):

1. The *Auto* begins in the heavenly, spiritual level of Calisto's dream in scene one. The entire scene is a projection of Calisto's imagination, which exists entirely in the upper part of the body.

2. Calisto's suffering at the beginning of scene two remains at an abstract level, but with the tortured souls in purgatory replacing heavenly perfection as its predominant image. The *Auto* still takes place in the mental plane, but there is already a symbolic descent from heaven to purgatory. This abstract level ends when Calisto mentions Melibea to Sempronio for the first time (I, 93).

3. After Calisto and Sempronio discuss women and love on a theoretical level, Calisto describes Melibea's specific virtues, family background, and mental qualities.

4. As Calisto's discussion shifts from Melibea's spiritual *virtudes* to her physical *hermosura,* his description begins with her golden hair and beautiful face and progressively descends to her small breasts. Calisto specifically mentions that he cannot describe her lower body, which he calls "lo occulto" (I, 100).

5. At the close of scene two, Sempronio mentions Celestina as an expert on the lower body stratum, and Calisto's attention becomes completely fixed on this physical and material level.

6. When Celestina arrives at Calisto's house, the young protagonist lies prostrate on the ground at her feet, showing how he has descended to the same earthly level as the old bawd.

The first part of Calisto's descent is the transition between the *Auto*'s first two scenes. Before and after the dream, Calisto exists in an ideal and abstract space whose dominant metaphors are heaven and purgatory. During Calisto's imaginary conversation at the beginning of the *Auto,* Calisto affirms that his pleasure before Melibea's vision is greater than that of the saints in God's presence:

> ¿Quién vido en esta vida cuerpo glorificado de ningún hombre como agora el mío? Por cierto, los gloriosos santos que se deleytan en la visión divina no gozan más que yo agora en el acatamiento tuyo. Mas, o triste, que en esto diferimos, que ellos puramente se glorifican sin temor de caer de tal bienaventurança, y yo, misto, me alegro con recelo del esquivo tormento que tu absencia me ha de causar. (I, 86)

The principal imagery of this passage – with the *cuerpo glorificado* and the *gloriosos santos [que] se glorifican* – is the glory of God in heavenly paradise. The *cuerpo glorificado* refers to the spiritual body that is reunited with the disembodied soul in God's presence during the resurrection of the dead. The *visión divina* represents the beatific experience of the eternal union with God that the *gloriosos santos* start to enjoy at the moment of death.[4] All of Calisto's impressions of ecstacy are celestial and immaterial in nature, and although he recognizes that his joy is temporary, he also indicates that he would not trade the saints' heavenly bliss for the vision of Melibea that he is presently witnessing: "[E]n verdad, si Dios me diesse en el cielo la silla sobre sus santos, no lo ternía por tanta felicidad" (I, 87).

Calisto becomes despondent once his vision of Melibea vanishes, but his expression of suffering in scene two maintains the same incorporeal character as his previous representation of ecstacy. Calisto believed that his vision of Melibea was superior to heaven, but his present suffering is far worse than purgatory: "Por cierto si el [fuego] del purgatorio es tal, más querría que mi spíritu fuesse con los de los brutos animales que por medio de aquél yr a la gloria de los santos" (I, 92). With the figurative descent from heaven into purgatory, Calisto's feelings remain within a non-physical plane that maintains an absolute separation between vision and reality. When Sempronio asks how the fire that burns within him is greater than the fire that burned Rome, Calisto explains that,

> ... mayor es la llama que dura ochenta años que la que en un día passa, y mayor la que mata un ánima que la que quema cient mil cuerpos. Como de la aparencia a la existencia, como de lo bivo a lo pintado, como de la sombra a lo real, tanta diferencia ay del fuego que dizes al que me quema. (I, 92)

Calisto indicates that the strongest pain affects the *ánima* instead of the body, so the worst kind of suffering is that of the *almas en pena* while they are in purgatory. Once again, Calisto is expressing himself in incorporeal images. The contrast between appearance and existence, the living and the painted, and the shadow and the real underlines Calisto's central conflict between the uncertain reality that surrounds him and the vision of Melibea that haunts him. He can see the young woman in his imagination, but he cannot bridge the gap that separates this vision from physical reality. Calisto takes the first step in his descent from purgatory to an earthly world when he finally mentions to Sempronio the cause of

---

[4] See Corcoran and Redle on the glorified body and the beatific vision.

his malady: he is not a Christian, but rather, "Melibeo só, y a Melibea adoro, y en Melibea creo, y a Melibea amo" (I, 93).

Now that Calisto has brought the problem out into the open, he and Sempronio are free to discuss and describe Melibea, although the young woman never makes a direct appearance in the *Auto*. Our knowledge of Melibea in the primitive text exists exclusively in the verbal plane because we see her only within Calisto's imagination and descriptions. Just as in Calisto's dream, we can see that the Melibea in the primitive text is a clear extension of Calisto's personality:

> SEMPRONIO. Lo primero eres hombre y de claro ingenio, y más, a quien la natura dotó de los mejores bienes que tuvo, conviene a saber: hermosura, gracia, grandeza de miembros, fuerça, ligereza, y allende desto, fortuna medianamente partió contigo lo suyo en tal quantidad que los bienes que tienes de dentro con los de fuera resplandecen...
> CALISTO. [E]n todo lo que me has gloriado, Sempronio, sin proporción ni comparación se aventaja Melibea. Miras la nobleza y antigüedad de su linaje, el grandísimo patrimonio, el excelentísimo ingenio, las resplandecientes virtudes, la altitud y ineffable gracia, la soberana hermosura.... (I, 99-100)

While Calisto believes that Melibea outdoes him in all areas, his description underlines the similarities between the two of them. Both Calisto and Melibea are distinguished by their *ingenio,* their *gracia,* and their *hermosura,* although Calisto affirms that these qualities are far superior in Melibea. The young woman is literally a projection and amplification of Calisto because the entire concept exists solely within Calisto's imagination. Unfortunately, Sempronio reveals in an aside that Calisto's reporting is absurd and unreliable, so the reader cannot truly know about Melibea from the information contained in the *Auto:* "(¡Qué mentiras y qué locuras dirá agora este cativo de mi amo!)" (I, 100). Sempronio realizes that Calisto views the outside world with "ojos de allinde, con que lo poco pareçe mucho y lo pequeño grande" (I, 102), so we can place little stock in the *galán's* descriptions.

Calisto makes the final transition from the ethereal Melibea in the opening scene to a more physical Melibea in scene two when he describes the young woman in traditional descending order as a collection of *cabello, ojos, pestañas, nariz, dientes,* and *tetas.* Nevertheless, Calisto realizes that these descriptions are a pale substitute for an intimate, physical knowledge of Melibea, which would logically be the next step in this progression from the immaterial to the material sphere, and from the upper to the lower body. Calisto states that the only reason that he and Sempronio are talking about the theoretical Melibea is his lack of direct experience with the young woman. Any real contact with her would eliminate the need to describe her, so the physical world now takes clear precedence over the visual and verbal world: "Y lo que te dixere [de Melibea] será de lo descobierto, que si de lo occulto yo hablarte sopiera, no nos fuera necessario altercar tan miserablemente estas razones" (I, 100).[5] It is hard for him to describe the physical body, although his linguistic shortcomings make him all the more desirous of Melibea: "[L]a redondeza y forma de las pequeñas tetas, ¿quién te la podría figurar? Que se despereza el hombre quando las mira" (I, 101).

Calisto relies on visions and *razones* because he has no connection with his beloved Melibea, and apparently no way to reach her. Celestina becomes decisive for Calisto because she exists precisely within the lower physical plane that Calisto hopes to attain. Her business is literally *lo occulto,* as Calisto understands when Sempronio says that she has made and unmade 5,000 virgins in the city. Sempronio indicates that, "A las duras peñas promoverá y provocará a luxuria, si quiere" (I, 103), so she can make even inanimate objects exist within the sensual and physical sphere.

---

[5] Ernesto Veres d'Ocón (1951) has written that Don Quixote's description of Dulcinea, just as Calisto's account of Melibea, follows the traditional pattern of medieval rhetoric:

El orden de enumeración de los rasgos físicos es similar al de los retratos retóricos medievales, dividido claramente en cuatro momentos:

    a) Cualidades abstractas y encarecimiento de la hermosura.

    b) Cabeza y cara: los rasgos son descritos de arriba abajo.

    c) El resto del busto, partes del cuerpo visibles (manos) y aspecto general sintetizado en su blancura .

    d) Reticencia final. (252)

While the two descriptions follow the same pattern, there is an important difference with what Veres D'Ocón calls the "reticencia final." Don Quixote ends his description of Dulcinea by saying that, "y las partes que a la vista humana encubrió la honestidad son tales, según yo pienso y entiendo, que sólo la discreta consideración puede encarecerlas, y no compararlas" (I, 13, 121). Calisto's "no nos fuera necessario altercar tan miserablemente estas razones" (I, 100) is far removed from Don Quixote's "honestidad" and "discreta consideración." Moreover, Don Quixote ends his description with the "reticencia" while Calisto *begins* the report with this rhetorical device, a change from the medieval pattern that emphasizes that the whole description would be unnecessary if he had physical knowledge of Melibea.

Once Sempronio mentions Celestina, the tone of the *Auto* becomes firmly planted in the physical plane, in the same way that the mention of Melibea shifted the action from the immaterial to the descriptive level. Calisto has spent most of the first act in the isolation of his chamber on the second floor, but when he receives Celestina he comes down to the first floor in order to establish contact with her on ground level.[6] The upper floor represents an absolute separation from life on earth; it is a cerebral and hermetic place that stands totally apart from the fruitful and regenerative activity of the earthly stratum. Celestina, on the other hand, functions best in the degraded and reproductive terrestial sphere, so Calisto's descent indicates a literal rejection of all that is noble and abstract and a total acceptance of the vital life forces that exist exclusively within this earthly, material plane.

The lower bodily stratum, as personified by Celestina, gives Calisto new life and resurrects him from death as it becomes his figurative womb. Calisto and Celestina are not united in imaginary visions or in heaven, but literally on earth, *la tierra,* as Pármeno sadly notes: ("¡O Calisto desventurado, abatido, ciego! Y en tierra está adorando a la más antigua [y] puta tierra, que fregaron sus espaldas en todos los burdeles. Deshecho es, vencido es, caýdo es; no es capaz de ninguna redención ni consejo ni esfuerço") (I, 116-17). Now that Calisto is groveling *en tierra,* he is totally *ciego* and there will be no more visions or dreams in the *Auto,* although Fernando de Rojas returns to this theme at the beginning of act two. Calisto is happy to abandon his visions now that he believes that the old woman will deliver Melibea to him, and his previous sloth and inertia are overwhelmed by a level of frenetic activity that would have seemed impossible for Calisto a short time before.

Celestina produces a similar form of degradation in Pármeno, but the young servant is far less willing to abandon his ideals than his master. Pármeno makes a long and detailed description of a woman just as Calisto does, but it is about Celestina's negative traits rather than about Melibea's positive qualities. Calisto is anxious to reach the physical plane, but the younger and more inexperienced

---

[6] Celestina is the first to indicate that Calisto and Pármeno come down from the second floor: "(Passos oygo; acá descienden)" (I, 114). Pármeno then confirms this information: "De verte o de oýrte descender por la escalera [Celestina y Sempronio], parlan lo que éstos fingidamente han dicho..." (I, 115).

Pármeno still wavers between suspicion and acceptance. Pármeno wants to believe in the elevated concepts of honor and service, but that alternative is quite impossible for a servant whose own master does not recognize their importance. He tries to convince Calisto that he is a loyal servant – "Quéxome, Calisto, de la dubda de mi fidelidad y servicio" (I, 114) – but Calisto pays no attention to these concepts because of his overwhelming passion for Melibea.

Párameno's problem is that he tries to live in an idealized and imaginary world of his own creation rather than in the physical and conflictive world that surrounds him. When Párameno speaks with Celestina, it is evident that his youthful idealism is totally out of place in this earthy and degraded environment: "Pues yo . . . tengo por honesta cosa la pobreza alegre. . . . Querría passar la vida sin embidia, los yermos y aspereza sin temor, el sueño sin sobresaltos, las injurias con respuesta, las fuerças sin denuesto, las premias con resistencia" (I, 123). Párameno hopes to stay clear of the dynamic, chaotic world of grotesque realism, but that is precisely the sphere in which he finds himself, and he must now find his place in it.

The young man's mental concepts are as impermanent as Calisto's visions in the face of the physical onslaught of Celestina's world. She tells Párameno that there are only two conclusions that can be drawn from life, and they both deal with the physical world and the lower body instead of with ideals and ethics. First, Celestina says that men and women must love each other; second, "el que verdaderamente ama es necessario que se turbe con la dulçura del soberano deleyte, que por el hazedor de las cosas fue puesto" (I, 118). According to Celestina, the disorder of love is part of the natural order on earth, and it is impossible to try to stop such a powerful physical force. The theme of *deleyte* runs throughout the first act of *Celestina*, and it allows Celestina to bring Párameno down from his lofty ideals to the physical world of the lower body:

> CELESTINA. ¿Qué dirás a esto, Párameno? . . . Llégate acá, putico, que no sabes nada del mundo ni de sus deleytes. ¡Mas rabia mala me mate, si te llego a mí, aunque vieja! Que la boz tienes ronca, las barvas te apuntan; mal sosegadilla deves tener la punta de la barriga.
> PÁRMENO. ¡Como cola de alacrán!
> CELESTINA. Y aún peor, que la otra muerde sin hinchar, y la tuya hincha por nueve meses.
> PÁRMENO. ¡Hy, hy, hy! (I, 118)

Pármeno tries to resist Celestina, but his festive laughter indicates how easily the old woman subverts Pármeno's puerile self-image. Despite the young man's apparent rectitude, Pármeno is vulnerable before Celestina because he exists through borrowed speech and thoughts. Instead of imagining creative ideas and visions like Calisto, Pármeno repeats dignified thoughts that he has heard from others, but these concepts have little basis in reality and no relation to the environment that surrounds him: "O Celestina, *oýdo he a mis mayores* que un exemplo de luxuria o avaricia mucho mal haze" (our emphasis, I, 125).

Celestina degrades Pármeno by substituting her ideas for the ones he has previously heard and absorbed, and more importantly by interesting him in a new form of discourse based on physical *deleyte*. Instead of intellectual or moral concepts, Celestina tells Pármeno that he must talk of worldly pleasures, and that this form of speech comes about only through personal, sensual experience:

> El deleyte es con los amigos en las cosas sensuales, y especial en recontar las cosas de amores y comunicarlas. "Esto hize, esto otro me dixo; tal donayre passamos, de tal manera la tomé, assí la besé, assí me mordió, assí la abracé, assí se allegó. ¡O qué habla, o qué gracia, o qué juegos, o qué besos!.... ¿Cómo te fue? Cata el cornudo; sola la dexa. Dale otra buelta, tornemos allá". Y para esto Pármeno ¿ay deleyte sin compañía? Alahé, alahé, la que las sabe las tañe. Éste es el deleyte, que lo ál, mejor lo hazen los asnos en el prado. (I, 126)

Pármeno attempts to defend his belief in reasoned discourse by rejecting the earthly delights that Celestina offers, but it is a weak defense because he is now reeling from Celestina's verbal assault. It makes little sense for Pármeno to resist temptation when he has the point of his belly "como cola de alacrán" (I, 118), and when he readily admits that Areúsa "maravillosa cosa es" (I, 124). Like Calisto, Pármeno sees things with *ojos de allinde,* but it appears that these eyes are turned on himself as he tries to present a self-image that does not correspond to his own physical self. Pármeno objects that he does not wish to be invited to try these delights, yet it is quite clear that this *barbiponiente* suffers more from indecision than from moral qualms:

No querría, madre, me combidasses a consejo con amonestación de deleyte, como hizieron los que, caresciendo de razonable fundamiento, opinando hizieron sectas embueltas en dulce veneno para captar y tomar las voluntades de los flacos y con polvos de sabroso affecto cegaron los ojos de la razón. (I, 126).

Celestina's response to Pármeno is as explosive as it is definitive: "¿Qué es razón, loco? ¿Qué es affecto, asnillo?" (I, 126). Calisto has already said in the second scene that he and Sempronio "alterca[n] tan miserablemente estas razones" (I, 110) only because Calisto lacks direct experience with Melibea, but now Celestina rejects the possibility of reasoning all together. Elevated thoughts and idealized concepts have no importance when compared with direct experience in life, and this experience is completely closed off to a young man like Pármeno unless he joins forces with Celestina. With insufficient practical experience to fall back upon, Pármeno once again relies on borrowed ideas that now permit him to accept the old woman's tutelage: "(Oýdo he que deve hombre a sus mayores creer).... Por esso perdóname, háblame; que no sólo quiero oýrte y creerte, mas en singular merced recebir tu consejo.... Por esso, manda, que a tu mandado mi consentimiento se humilla" (I, 127-128).

Although Fernando de Rojas alters Pármeno's character in act two, by the end of the *Auto* Pármeno is firmly under Celestina's and Sempronio's control. He laughs when he learns that Calisto gave Celestina one hundred coins, and tells Sempronio that he is, "Como quisieres, aunque estoy espantado" (I, 129). Sempronio's response to Pármeno leaves little doubt that the *antiguo auctor* planned no further independent action from the young servant – "Pues calla, que yo te haré espantar dos tanto" (I, 129) – and that Pármeno was as much under Celestina's spell as his master.

The *Auto* moves from absolute disorder in scene one to a situation of order restored by the time Celestina leaves Calisto's house at the end of the primitive text. Calisto and Pármeno begin the story at an immaterial or theoretical level, but they are both brought down to the physical sphere through Celestina's earthly and sensual influence. The *Auto* emphasizes the inadequacy of the sterile description of Melibea reported by Calisto, which turns out to be no more than an inaccurate, cerebral monologue. For Celestina, true dialogue is the result of a direct, sensual experience that must be communicated to others because love is such a powerful force in the *Auto* that it ends up creating its own dialogic imperative.

The *Auto* progresses from the immaterial space of ideas and images to the physical space of the lower body and the senses. At the close of the primitive text, all four main characters operate on the same earthly and material plane, an area dominated and controlled by Celestina. They now live within an ordered chaos that seems to have found its own level of creative equilibrium while it celebrates its own dynamic activity. The *antiguo auctor* appears to believe that the characters should coexist in the lower body stratum, and it seems likely that the story would have progressed to a happy ending if it had maintained its original form. While Fernando de Rojas subverts these ideas when he creates a conflictive, tragic ending to the continuation of the book, the *Auto* manifests its spatial and thematic unity when it is read as an independent, interpolated text within *Celestina*.

III

TEMPORAL UNITY AND OBJECTIVE TIME IN *CELESTINA*

Celestina's temporal development has been a point of discussion for modern scholars for almost fifty years. Around the middle of this century, Stephen Gilman and Manuel J. Asensio began the debate on the role of time as a unifying element in the work. As we have noted in chapters one and two, the *Auto*'s opening scene apparently takes place during the text's first morning, but Rojas's continuation of the work suggests that Calisto's and Melibea's first meeting occurred several days before. Gilman (1945) believed that the apparent temporal contradictions between the *Auto* and the continuation were so extensive that Rojas could not have failed to see them. Gilman therefore concluded that this problem must have a logical explanation because Rojas would not leave such an obvious contradiction in the work: "Sabía [Rojas] intuitivamente que la entrega de Melibea, en los pocos días que le permitía la presentación dramática ininterrumpida, era artísticamente insostenible" (157).

Gilman tried to resolve the enigma by affirming that Rojas consciously created two different kinds of time in the work. First, there is an objective external time that develops when the characters indicate whether it is day or night, or that it is early or late in the day. Second, Gilman believes that *Celestina* has another form of time that progresses at a totally different rate from the external time: "[un] tiempo que funciona como tiempo, que progresa con el diálogo, aunque a una velocidad mucho mayor" (152). This second form of subjective or human time means that the work does not respect a linear temporal progression, which permits the author and the characters an autonomy of action free from time limits and constraints.

Asensio (1952) studies the same textual problems as Gilman, but he concludes that the principal problem is not the temporal sequence in *Celestina,* but rather modern critics' misreading of the work. Asensio agrees with Gilman that we need another explanation for the passing of time in *Celestina,* but he does not believe that the solution lies in attributing new and different temporal characteristics to the text. Asensio affirms that the work has an established and comprehensible temporal order that modern readers have not understood properly:

> En general, las ideas y teorías indicadas revelan un sincero deseo de salvar imaginadas tachas en la obra que todos admiran, cuyo comentario se hacía imprescindible para poder apreciar la manera en que las distintas soluciones afectaban a la esencia y significado de *La Celestina*. Muchos de esos errores parten, directa o indirectamente, de no hallarse despejada la incógnita del factor tiempo. El punto de partida para resolverla ha sido mi convencimiento de la visión íntegra y precisa que tenía Rojas del mundo que había creado. En el estudio interno de la obra creo encontrar profusión de pruebas de que fue concebida dentro de un tiempo lógico, concreto, real, en el cual los acontecimientos fluyen sin rebasarlo. (33)

Asensio's analysis is based on a simple yet important observation. He believes that after a crucial comment by Pármeno in the second act – "Señor, porque perderse el otro día el neblí fue causa de tu entrada en la huerta de Melibea a le buscar..." (II, 134-35) – then the reader understands that the first and only conversation between Calisto and Melibea takes place before the work's first day. There is no confusion in the characters' interpretation of the temporal sequence because Calisto has just referred to the passage of time when he asks, "Tú, Pármeno, ¿qué te parece de lo que oy ha passado?" (II, 133). According to Asensio, the characters cannot create a second, subjective time at the same moment they refer to the objective time that surrounds them. Asensio also observes that we cannot believe that Calisto met Melibea when he went hawking the first morning because Pármeno later indicates that his master does not have the habit of leaving the house early in the day (VIII, 213).

Asensio concludes that scene one of *Celestina* is in reality a prologue to the work that occurs some days before the rest of the text.

For Asensio, this idea agrees with the information that we derive from the characters' conversation, while also respecting the work's temporal development:

> Melibea, Calisto, Celestina, Sempronio y Pármeno, individual y conjuntamente, establecen la separación de la escena del huerto (Auto I), del resto de la acción;[1] escena que viene a constituir el Prólogo de la obra; los muchos días que median son bien concretos, como corresponde al curso normal del tiempo en toda la *Comedia*. (38)

Despite the many important observations in Asensio's article, Gilman (1953) rejects the possibility of a new interpretation of *Celestina*'s temporal structure. Gilman criticizes Asensio's effort to find a simple and reasonable solution to the problem of time in the work, which suggests that Gilman believes that *Celestina* requires a complicated temporal development:

> It is, however, disconcerting to learn that Professor Asensio proposes, instead of a more satisfactory interpretation, the non-existence of any temporal contradiction. Indeed, he seems to take as a point of departure the assumption that, since two separate times cannot logically coexist, literally they must not exist, and he proceeds with diligence to reconcile the opposed necessities. (42)

Asensio's response to Gilman (1953) repeats the idea that a prologue or initial separation is the most logical interpretation that we have for scene one of *Celestina*. Asensio reiterates his belief that it is preferable to have a logical interpretation that respects the author's text and sensibilities than to create an interpretation that does not agree with the book's literary reality:

> Mi punto de partida era la visión íntegra y precisa que el autor tenía de su obra, por lo que no es de extrañar no me satisficiera la teoría del profesor Gilman que, aparte de sus contradicciones, negaba a Rojas una clara percepción de la esencia de su propia creación; y cuando, ahora, el señor Gilman se declara descontento de ella, ni veo dos tiempos ni la necesidad de ellos. (46)

---

[1] See chapter 1, n. 1, for the additional textual references that indicate that Calisto and Melibea's meeting occurs before the beginning of the book.

In a later book, Gilman (1956) emphasizes the importance of the passing of time and the fundamental contrast between day and night in *Celestina*. Gilman studies the role of time in *Celestina* and how this temporal progression creates a comprehensible structure for the development of the plot and the action. Nevertheless, he perhaps contradicts himself and weakens his own argument when he combines this objective time frame with his second interpretation of subjective time in *Celestina*:

> A curious betrayal of this central conflict is Rojas' failure to equate the duration of the individual life with external time – with what Thibaudet calls the "durée commune," measurable by the church bells and darkness noticed in the dialogue. As early as Act II when the sequence of speech and event is still unbroken by nightfall, Parmeno speaks of Calisto's encounter with Melibea as occurring "el otro día." And by Act X, when just one day has been registered in action, Melibea remembers "muchos e muchos días" as having gone by since "esse noble caballero me habló en amor." Just as Calisto in his soliloquy converts one or two sentences of Melibea (as transcribed in the dialogue of Act XIV) into an almost limitless duration of delightful hesitancy, so a little more than twenty-four hours may correspond to an experience so timeless that it can only be expressed as "many days." (146)

Despite the sometimes acerbic disagreement between Gilman and Asensio, each scholar makes an important contribution to the study of time in *Celestina*. Gilman studies the many contradictory temporal references in the work and understands that we need a new explanation for the book's temporal progression that goes beyond the previous psychological and moral studies of the different characters. Asensio comprehends that although Gilman presents the question correctly, the solution for this problem must be logical and reasonable, and should be based on the proper interpretation of the book's opening scene.

As part of her study of time in *Celestina*, María Rosa Lida de Malkiel (1962) analyzes the repeated temporal references in act one, but within "la correlación impresionista y no objetiva de hechos dados en la *Tragicomedia*" (175). Lida de Malkiel believes that the apparent temporal contradictions in *Celestina* do not represent a defect in the book because she has a solution for the subjective time that she sees in Rojas's work:

> Pienso que es pecado de injusticia contra los excelsos autores de la *Tragicomedia* concebir tal insistencia en el tiempo implícito como una falla mecánica..., como una estrategema – no un recurso artístico constante – empleada una sola vez para salir del atolladero (Asensio) o como una insuficiente conciencia de género literario (Gilman, 1945) o como una incapacidad de igualar el tiempo como duración psicológica con el tiempo como dimensión física (Gilman, 1956). No es lícito presumir error mientras quede a mano explicación que muestre propósito coherente en ese peculiarísimo proceder. (176)

Lida de Malkiel attempts to resolve the problem of *Celestina*'s psychological and temporal realism with the affirmation that a certain amount of time has passed between the first and second scenes of act one. According to Lida, the text permits the existence of actions that are "simultáneas sin ser verosímilmente coextensivas en el tiempo" (181), so the action can develop within an unorthodox time frame that only has the appearance of a normal temporal progression:

> Una importante consecuencia se desprende de este rasgo: por demorada que sea, la acción de la *Tragicomedia* no representa compactamente lo que pasa desde que el neblí de Calisto penetra en el jardín de Melibea. Otras pruebas confirman el hecho de que los autores no se propusieron representar una secuencia naturalísticamente completa, por más que el comer, dormir, anochecer o amanecer que sirven de jalones den la ilusión de que todo se desarrolla a la vista del espectador ideal. (178)

Dorothy Sherman Severin (1970) also studies the function of time in *Celestina*, but within the Aristotelian concept of motion, "[W]here Aristotelian 'motion' includes movement through what we would now call both space and time" (45). Severin, much like Lida de Malkiel, attempts to show that the apparent contradictions studied by Gilman and Asensio, among others, have a logical explanation as part of the characters' subjective viewpoint towards the passing of time:

> The paradoxical "times" of *La Celestina*, which have been seen as a clash between external dimension (the four-day action of the work) and internal duration (the much longer psychological process of the love affair), are resolved when they become a function

of motion. Rojas as author cannot catalogue every moment of the physical and psychological development of the love affair; instead he gives us a sampling of both. Although he seemingly presents an unbroken sequence of events, we realize that this surface unity is illusory; while maintaining the illusion of continuous surface motion he is in fact giving us a sampling of both physical and psychological motion and time which extends over a month or more. (45)

Severin searches for an explanation for the apparent temporal contradictions in *Celestina*, but it is obvious that there can be no resolution of the enigma unless we properly locate the book's first scene in space and time. Severin, much like Lida de Malkiel, has difficulty explaining the supposed temporal separation between scenes one and two of *Celestina*. Despite the insistence that the work contains some form of subjective time, neither Lida nor Severin properly establish why there would be so many subjective days between the book's first two scenes, nor do they create a logical argument for this position.

Although subjective time no longer receives much critical attention, modern scholars still lack a clear idea of how time works in *Celestina*. Charles F. Fraker (1990) writes that, "[O]ne must confess that the chronology of the work is never very clear" (18), and reiterates that, "The sequence of time in *Celestina* is never wholly clear" (58). Miguel Marciales (1985) believes that that the first act has "cierta unidad, si exceptuamos la [primera escena]" (I, 70). James R. Stamm (1988) studies the different temporal structures that he sees in the *Auto* and in Rojas's continuation of *Celestina*, and accepts Asensio's idea that *Celestina*'s opening scene is a dramatic prologue to the rest of the work. According to Stamm, "Uno de los grandes alcances del Antiguo Auctor [en el primer acto] es precisamente el de idear una estructura no aristotélica, no cronológica, no anclada en lugares y tiempos concretos y determinados" (63). Although the opening scene "existe prácticamente fuera del tiempo" (62), the rest of the *Comedia* takes place during four clearly defined days (177-78).

There are additional questions about the interpretation of time in Severin's and Maite Cabello's edition of *Celestina*, which was originally published in 1987. During the work's first evening in act seven, Pármeno reminds Celestina about his interest in the young prostitute Areúsa. Celestina tells Pármeno that she has been working on this problem, and that the young woman will soon be his: "Si te lo prometí, no lo he olvidado, ni creas que he perdido con los años la memoria. Que más de tres xaques ha recibido de mí sobre ello en tu absencia. Ya creo que stará bien madura...." (VII, 200). Severin y Cabello write that Celestina's response indicates that time does not follow a logical sequence in the book: "Si la secuencia temporal en *La Celestina* fuera realista, Areúsa no hubiera podido ser recordada a Pármeno por Celestina, ya que, por lo que sabemos, aquél no había tenido oportunidad de verla" (VII, 200, n. 20).

These comments by Severin and Cabello represent a possible misreading of the text. Although Celestina may exaggerate the number of times it has occurred, what happens in the work is that the old woman speaks to Areúsa about Pármeno outside of the text, and not to Pármeno about Areúsa.[2] Time develops in a perfectly logical fashion because this brief conversation leads directly to next scene, where Celestina speaks to Areúsa in the young prostitute's bedroom: "Ya sabes lo que de Pármeno te ove dicho; quéxaseme que aún verle no quieres" (VII, 204).

Severin and Cabello make a second comment about the passing of time in the footnotes to act ten. Melibea, now desperate for Calisto's love, confesses to Celestina that, "Muchos y muchos días son passados que esse noble cavallero me habló en amor; tanto me fue entonces su habla enojosa quanto después que tú me lo tornaste a nombrar, alegre" (X, 245). Severin and Cabello write that, "De nuevo, el espacio de tiempo percibido por los personajes no se corresponde con el percibido por el lector" (X, 245, n. 17). Therefore Severin and Cabello, much like Gilman, Asensio, Lida, Marciales, and Stamm, base their analysis of the temporal sequence in *Celestina* on the idea that the book's first scene does not occur during the first day of the narration.[3] Despite the nuances that distinguish their different interpretations, these critics have written long and serious studies based on the standard analysis of a conversation between Calisto and Melibea that is particularly difficult and contradictory for the modern reader.

---

[2] For the correct interpretation of this scene, see María Rosa Lida de Malkiel (1962: 176) and James R. Stamm (104-05).

[3] For an innovative and important opposing viewpoint, see A. Rumeau (1966) and Marcel Bataillon (9-17).

As we have noted in the first two chapters of this study, the opening scene of *Celestina* appears to be a dream or vision that takes place in Calisto's bedroom during the work's first morning. Instead of the apparent temporal problems analyzed by traditional critics, Calisto's dream suggests that Rojas's original sixteen-act *Comedia* occurs during a clearly delineated time frame.[4] There is no contradiction between the characters' subjective and external times because whenever they refer to the first meeting between Calisto and Melibea – whether it be "el otro día" (II, 164), "muchos días" before (XII, 164), or "quántos días antes de agora" (X, 247) – it is understood that it occurs before the beginning of the work. According to this interpretation, Calisto sends Sempronio for Celestina early in the morning of the first day, and the old woman pays her first visit to Melibea that afternoon. Night falls after Celestina's return to Calisto's house, and the first day ends in act seven when Pármeno spends the evening with Areúsa.

The second day begins in act eight when Pármeno awakens and returns to Calisto's house, where he affirms his newfound loyalty to Sempronio. Act twelve represents the evening of the second day and the pre-dawn hours of the third day. During this brief period, Calisto visits Melibea for the first time, and shortly thereafter Celestina, Pármeno, and Sempronio are killed. Calisto spends the evening of the third day of the *Comedia* in Melibea's garden in act fourteen, and he falls to his death just before daybreak. It is already light outside when Melibea kills herself, so seventy-two hours have passed from the beginning to the end of the sixteen-act *Comedia*. The book begins in Calisto's chamber while he bemoans his love for Melibea, and it ends in Pleberio's room as he bemoans his love for the same young woman.

---

[4] Garci Gómez (1987) later writes that, "En ese artículo [1985] creo haber explicado satisfactoriamente la razón de por qué se refieren al 'otro día' Pármeno y, más adelante, Melibea... cuestión que tanto parecía preocupar, entre otros, a Stephen Gilman; según éste, los personajes hablaban de haber pasado días, donde de acuerdo con sus propios cálculos se había dado intervalo de 'a lo sumo... cinco o seis horas' (*'La Celestina': Arte y Estructura* [Madrid, Taurus, 1974], 341). En el meticuloso estudio del tiempo que el autor hace en las páginas siguientes se demuestra cómo en la mente de Rojas – expresada por boca de diversos personajes – habían transcurrido varios días desde aquel primer encuentro en el huerto – al que alude Pármeno – y la primera escena en la alcoba, con la que comenzaba su obrita 'el antiguo autor' " (11, n. 4).

The temporal development of the *Comedia* is so well laid out that the four periods betwen midnight and the early morning produce most of the important events in the book. First, we meet Calisto and see the love problem that will drive the action during the entire text. That evening, Pármeno has his first sexual experience in act seven, which unites him with Sempronio and eventually produces both of their deaths. After midnight of the second day, Calisto visits Melibea outside of her window in act twelve, and soon afterward Celestina, Párimeno, and Sempronio die shortly before daybreak. Finally, at the end of the third day, Calisto and Melibea fall to their deaths at Pleberio's house just before and after sunrise.[5]

When Sosia says that Sempronio and Párimeno "madrugaron a morir" (XIII, 277-78), in reality he could say the same about all of the deaths in the book. The sixteen acts of *La comedia de Calisto y Melibea* are not characterized by an irregular or subjective temporal development, but rather by a very well organized and precise temporal structure with divisions of twenty-four hours that separate the text's four most important periods. Within this structured time frame, there is no room for multiple temporal progressions or subjective time. As Asensio anticipated at the beginning of the nineteen fifties, the passage of time in *Celestina* must be simple, logical, and relatively realistic, and the only thing needed was a new interpretation that would explain the temporal development in precisely this fashion.

The characters in *Celestina* are aware of the passing of time and make repeated efforts to speed up or slow down the action in the text, but they are invariably unsuccessful in their efforts. Despite the traditional belief in subjective time, we will demonstrate that the temporal development is outside of the characters' control, and that the deaths in *Celestina* are caused in part by the characters' inability to understand and direct the progress of events in time. Time evolves in a straightforward and objective fashion throughout *Celestina*, and despite the characters' incessant activity, the work's temporal progression invariably defeats all of their efforts to change the future. We will support this position by studying the role and structure of time in the original sixteen-act *Comedia,* and by analyzing how each of the five main characters interprets and reacts to the progression of time around him.

---

[5] Stamm has a similar analysis of the temporal movement in the *Comedia,* but he separates the opening scene as a *Prólogo Dramático* (177-78).

Of all the characters in the book, Calisto is the most unaware of the importance of time in the novel. He wishes to separate himself from the physical world at the beginning of the work, but once Sempronio tells him about Celestina, then Calisto's sloth is transformed into a desperate rush to bring the old woman to his house. Later, when he learns from Celestina that Melibea reciprocates his love, he again withdraws to his bedroom and temporarily removes himself from the passing of time. He later becomes anxious about the time in the moments before his first visit to Melibea's house, wishing for the clock to quickly strike twelve. Finally, in the last day before his death, he is ensconced in his room repeating Melibea's words in an effort to recapture the immediate past and negate the passing of time.

The first to comment on Calisto's inconsistent character is Sempronio, who does not understand his master's sudden alteration during the book's first morning: "¡O desventura, o súbito mal! ¿Quál fue tan contrario acontescimiento que ansí tan presto robó el alegría deste hombre, y lo que peor es, junto con ella el seso?" (I, 89). Sempronio's words suggest that Calisto is bothered by something that has just taken place, which supports Garci-Gómez's idea that there is no temporal separation between the first two scenes in the book. But since the "contrario acontecimiento" is Calisto's vision, the servant does not know how to react to his master's unexpected peevishness. Sempronio therefore decides to let some time pass before he enters Calisto's room in order to see if this will calm his master:

> Con todo quiérole dexar un poco desbrave, madure, que oýdo he dezir que es peligro abrir o apremiar las postemas duras, porque más se enconan. Esté un poco, dexemos llorar al que dolor tiene. . . . Por esso quiérome soffrir un poco, si entretanto se matare, muera. (I, 89-90)

Sempronio's waiting cannot help Calisto because the young master never establishes a synchronous relation with external events. Calisto is in either too much of a hurry to get things done or is completely oblivious to the passing of time, so time cannot solve the problems of this essentially anachronic character. Sempronio tells Calisto that as far as women are concerned, he should be in a hurry only for the momentary physical pleasure that they bring him: "¡O qué plaga, o qué enojo, o qué fastío es conferir con ellas, más de aquel breve tiempo, que aparejadas son a deleyte!" (I, 98). Nevertheless, Calisto spends more time thinking and dreaming about his beloved than actually being with her before his death.

Once Sempronio decides to take advantage of his master's love for Melibea, he does all he can to fan Calisto's passions. Pármeno, on the other hand, attempts to have the opposite effect on his master. He explains to Calisto that his love for Melibea is a passing fancy, and that he should let time cool his passions rather than worsen the situation by listening to Sempronio:

> [Q]uitarse ha el velo de la ceguedad; passarán estos momentáneos fuegos; conozcerás mis agras palabras ser mejores para matar este fuerte cánçre que las blandas de Sempronio que lo cevan, atizan tu fuego, abivan tu amor, encienden tu llama, añaden astillas que tenga que gastar, hasta ponerte en la sepoltura. (II, 136)

Despite Pármeno's good intentions, his lack of maturity and experience makes it easy for Calisto to ignore his advice. Calisto's haste continues until Celestina returns from Melibea's house – "Madre mía, o abrevia tu razón o toma esta spada y mátame" (V, 177) – but it ends as quickly as it began once he understands that his love for Melibea is not as hopeless as he feared:

> Agora, señora, que me as dado seguro para que ose esperar todos los rigores de la respuesta, di quanto mandares y como quisieres, que yo estaré atento. Ya me reposa el coraçón; ya descansa mi pensamiento; ya reciben las venas y recobran su perdido sangre, ya he perdido temor; ya tengo alegría. Subamos, si mandas, arriba. En mi cámara me dirás por estenso lo que aquí he sabido en suma. (VI, 179-80)

This chamber is Calisto's natural habitat because it is a place where he can confuse night and day, and therefore create the illusion that time is not progressing around him. He exists almost entirely in the darkness, but he suffers a horrible death in the same darkness that he thought would provide his safety and comfort in a contrary world. If the darkness is a symbol of an atemporal place, a void where Calisto can relive his thoughts and conversations with

Melibea, then his dark death demonstrates the futiliy of the characters' attempts to alter the passing of time to their benefit.

Although Calisto repeatedly ignores Pármeno's advice, the young servant demonstrates from the beginning of the work that he is adept at using time to his advantage. Pármeno wants to use his experience with Celestina to malign the procuress in Calisto's eyes, but his arguments have an evident drawback because they involve him directly in the old woman's evil history. Pármeno's only recourse is to consciously or unconsciously use time as a palliative for his own dishonorable background:

> Saberlo has [, señor]. Días grandes son passados que mi madre, mujer pobre, morava en su vezindad, la qual rogada por esta Celestina, me dio a ella por serviente, aunque ella no me conosce, por lo poco que la serví y por la mudança que la edad ha hecho. . . . Pero de aquel poco tiempo que la serví, recogía la nueva memoria lo que la vieja no ha podido quitar. (I, 109-10)

With this explanation, Pármeno attempts to create a temporal separation between his life and Celestina's, emphasizing that "días grandes son passados" since the time he was her servant. He also stresses "lo poco que la serví" so that Calisto will not imagine that he has been contaminated by Celestina's poisonous influence. In Pármeno's mind, the little time that he spent with Celestina and the long time that has passed since then are enough to wipe out the vestiges of his past.

Unfortunately for him, this assumption backfires when he tells Celestina who he is: "¿Quién [soy]? Párneno, hijo de Alberto tu compadre, que estuve contigo un mes que te me dio mi madre, quando moravas a la cuesta del río cerca de las tenerías" (I, 120).[6] Celestina immediately understands that these innocent memories have no relation with Párneno's true background. The young servant is the son of Claudina, who was "tan puta vieja" as Celestina (I, 120), and she never lets him forget it. Párneno changes his memory of the past in order to emphasize his own innocence, but this past reasserts itself to destroy the illusions that he has created.

---

[6] The *Tragicomedia* changes this sentence to, "que estuve contigo *poco tiempo* que te me dio mi madre, quando moravas a la cuesta del río cerca de las tenerías" (I, 120).

With his fictitious reconstruction of the past, Pármeno can say at first that, "Amo a Calisto porque le devo fidelidad por criança, por beneficios, por ser dél honrrado y bien tratado, que es la mayor cadena que el amor del servidor al servicio del señor prende, quanto lo contrario aparta" (I, 118). Celestina, however, tells Pármeno that times have changed and that he must realize that he lives in a conflictive age far removed from his youthful dreams:

> Reposa en alguna parte. ¿Y dónde mejor que en mi voluntad, en mi ánimo, en mi consejo, a quien tus padres te remetieron? ... dexa los vanos prometimientos de los señores, los quales deshechan la sustancia de sus sirvientes con huecos y vanos prometimientos.... Estos señores deste tiempo más aman assí que a los suyos, y no yerran; los suyos ygualmente lo deven hazer. Perdidas son las mercedes, las manificencias, los actos nobles. (I, 121-22)

Celestina emphasizes that Pármeno has old-fashioned ideas about servants and masters, and that he is foolish to think about service for masters who have no concept of responsibility towards their servants. According to Celestina, Pármeno is every bit as asynchronous as his master Calisto, but in a different way. Calisto cannot tell the time of day, while Pármeno is unable to recognize the societal changes that have taken place around him. He cannot live an idealized existence because time has destroyed the remnants of an honorable feudal society, leaving each person to watch out for his own interests.

Once Pármeno accepts that Calisto does not appreciate him, he begins to proclaim the importance of his own prehistory. The young man attempted to change his past and insist on how much time had gone by since he first knew Celestina, but he now boasts of his past service for the old woman and the positive effects it has had on his life: "Agora doy por bienempleado el tiempo que siendo niño te serví, pues tanto fruto trae para la mayor edad. Y rogaré a Dios por el alma de mi padre que tal tutriz me dexó, y de mi madre que a tal mujer me encomendó" (VII, 196)

Pármeno thus admits that that time does not allow the characters to escape their destinies. Pármeno has been unable to take advantage of the passing of time since he now rejoins the same unsavory social element that he belonged to when he was a boy. Like all of the other characters, he believes that he has been able to save himself just in time – "Di madrina [de Celestina], que es más cierto. Assí que quien a buen árbol se arrima.... Tarde fuy, pero temprano recaudé" (VIII, 216) – but in reality what he has done is to assure his own destruction: .

Sempronio is another character who thinks he can control and benefit from the passing of time. Sempronio's first attempt to alter the perception of time is the ruse he creates with Celestina to steal money from his master. When he goes to Celestina's house to tell her about Calisto's love for Melibea, the servant and the procuress are both in a hurry to begin the affair:

> SEMPRONIO. Madre mía, bien ternás confiança y creerás que no te burlo. Toma el manto y vamos, que por el camino sabrás lo que si aquí me tardase en dezir[te], impidiría tu provecho y el mío....
> CELESTINA. Pero di, no te detengas, que la amistad que entre ti y mí se affirma no ha menester preámbulos ni correlarios ni aparejos para ganar voluntad. Abrevia y ven al hecho, que vanamente se dize por muchas palabras lo que por pocas se puede entender. (I, 106, 107)

At first, Sempronio and Celestina are planning a very simple deception, but this plan inadvertently establishes the basis of their later conflict. Sempronio's economic interest lies in a group affair rather than in a solo effort, but despite her words in act one Celestina will not accept this condition for long. Sempronio tells Celestina:

> Calisto arde en amores de Melibea; de ti y de mí tiene necessidad. Pues juntos nos ha menester, juntos nos aprovechamos, que conoscer el tiempo y usar el hombre de la oportunidad haze los hombres prósperos. (I, 107)

Celestina and Sempronio face an opportunity that they cannot let slip through their fingers, and the old woman proposes to take advantage of Calisto's ailment by extending the love affair as long as possible in order to maximize the financial gain for both of them:

> Digo que me alegro destas nuevas, como los cirurjanos de los descalabrados; y como aquéllos dañan en los principios las llagas, y encarescen el prometimiento de la salud, ansí entiendo yo

hazer a Calisto. Alargarle he la certinidad del remedio, porque como dizen, el esperança luenga aflige el coraçón, y quanto él la perdiere, tanto gela promete. ¡Bien me entiendes! (I, 107)

Sempronio is naturally delighted with Celestina's plan to lengthen the love affair because he wants to continue in Calisto's employment while stealing from his master. Celestina initially wants to include even Pármeno in the deal, but she quickly realizes that the affair is much larger than it originally appeared to be. Calisto represents Celestina's last chance to make a significant amount of money in her final days, so she tries to change the temporal and participatory nature of their ruse, which produces a violent reaction from Pármeno and Sempronio.

It would seem illogical for Celestina to alter a plan that she herself has created, but the passing of time has had a tremendous effect on her and on the way she practices her profession. When Pármeno first talks to Calisto about Celestina in the *Auto*, the old woman appears to generate a frenetic level of activity that encompasses the life of the entire town. In Rojas's continuation, Celestina recalls how important she once was, but it is obvious that with her advancing years she is no longer the same person she was in her youth. She has aged so much that Melibea does not recognize her during their first meeting, even though it has only been two years since she last saw her former neighbor: "Vieja te has parado; bien dizen que los días no [se] van embalde ... otra paresces; muy mudada estás" (IV, 157).

The tremendous changes brought about by time have left Celestina with a great longing for the halcyon days when she played an active and profitable role in the town, but now she suffers the constant fight against grinding poverty and old age. Time has passed, and it has brought nothing but destruction in its wake:

> Mundo es, passe, ande su rueda, rodee sus alcaduces, unos llenos, otros vazíos. Ley es de fortuna que ninguna cosa en un ser mucho tiempo permanesce; su orden es mudanças. No puedo dezir sin lágrimas la mucha honrra que entonces tenía, aunque por mis pecados y mala dicha, poco a poco ha venido en diminución. Como declinavan mis días, assí se disminuya y menguava mi provecho.... Cerca ando de mi fin. En esto veo que me queda poca vida. (IX, 234)

This may be the only time that the main characters in *Celestina* admit the inevitability of the passing of time, and that this progression is completely out of their control. The characters talk about time and try to hurry it up or slow it down, but here Celestina realizes that it is useless to resist time's inexorable movement towards death and despair.

The years that have affected Celestina's physical appearance and left her in dire poverty have also changed the way she practices her profession. Despite her rush when she leaves her house with Sempronio in act one, she starts to slow down once she receives the one hundred coins from Calisto. Her age has sapped her energy and left her a tired, old woman, as Sempronio observes: "¡Qué spacio lleva la barbuda; menos sosiego trayan sus pies a la venida! A dineros pagados, braços quebrados. ¡Ce, señora Celestina, poco as aguijado!" (III, 138). Sempronio's comment is the first suggestion that Celestina may have trouble meeting the responsibilities that once were commonplace for her. She is hesitant and even fearful on the way to see Melibea, which is the exact opposite of what one would expect based on her former reputation in the city.

In the moments before she sees Melibea, Celestina and Sempronio talk about lengthening the amount of time the love affair will last because they still believe that they have control over the passage of time in the work:

> SEMPRONIO. Procuremos provecho mientra pendiere la contienda; y si a pie enxuto le pudiéremos remediar, lo mejor mejor es; y si no, poco a poco le soldaremos el reproche o menosprecio de Melibea contra él. Donde no, más vale que pene el amo al que no peligre el moço.
> CELESTINA. Bien as dicho; contigo stoy. Agradado me as; no podemos errar. (III, 141)

Sempronio's statement reveals that there is some danger involved for the servants, but he mistakenly thinks that time will permit him an easy escape from his problems. In the same way that Pármeno believes that he joins Celestina in the nick of time, Sempronio thinks that once they initiate the love affair between Calisto and Melibea, they can delay or even stop the chain of events that they have set in motion:

> Parece por tu razón que nos puede venir a nosotros daño deste negocio y quemarnos con las centellas que resultan deste fuego de Calisto.... Al primer desconcierto que vea en este negocio no como más su pan; más vale perder lo servido, que la vida por cobrallo; el tiempo me dirá qué haga, que primero que cayga del todo dará señal, como casa que se acuesta.... Que no ay cosa tan difícile de sufrir en sus principios, que el tiempo no la ablande y haga comportable. Ninguna llaga tanto se sintió que por luengo tiempo no afloxasse su tormento, ni plazer tan alegre fue que no le amengüe su antigüedad. (III, 140)

Sempronio considers time to be a natural ally because it will cool Calisto's ardor while preserving their economic benefit as long as possible. There is no indication of the tragedy that awaits them because of the unfounded belief that time's open nature will offer ample notice of future events. Pármeno's comments about the house falling are of course ironic because he will fall from a house precisely when he should be the one who "se acuesta."

Shortly before his death, Sempronio realizes that events are rushing towards a violent resolution, but then it is too late for him to escape. But during the first day, Sempronio still believes that time slows things down and brings them to a manageable level, which means that time is responsible for keeping order in the characters' lives:

> El mal y el bien, la prosperidad y adversidad, la gloria y pena, todo pierde con el timpo la fuerça de su acelerado principio. Pues los casos de admiración, y venidos con gran desseo, tan presto como passados, olvidados. Cada día vemos novedades y las oymos y las passamos.... [pero] a tres días passados o a la segunda vista no ay quien dello se maraville. (III, 140-41)

There is a further irony to Sempronio's words because in three days the town will surely marvel at the deaths of *Celestina*'s five main characters. The passing of time does not lead to a loss of public consciousness, but rather focuses the town's attention on their illicit activities.

The first instance that time becomes a point of conflict is when Celestina returns to Calisto's house after visiting Melibea. She has now learned that the affair will be far easier and far more profitable than she ever imagined: "Pues alégrate, vieja, que más sacarás deste pleyto que de quinze virgos que renovaras" (V, 171). Celestina quickly forgets about sharing her gain with the servants, believing that "mi mucha astucia" (V, 171) dominated the scene with Melibea. For the first time in many years, her experience appears to provide her with the success that would have eluded her younger competitors: "¡O quántas erraran en lo que yo he acertado! ¿Qué hizieran en tan fuerte estrecho estas nuevas maestras de mi officio sino responder algo a Melibea por donde se perdiera quanto yo con buen callar he ganado?" (V, 171-72).

For a brief moment, Celestina is rejuvenated after the unexpected opportunity with Melibea, and her previous sloth and self-doubt disappear as she tries to make a quick strike at Calisto's wealth. Her new attitude is reflected in the way she carries herself, which Sempronio immediately notices. Celestina literally curses her skirts for slowing her down as she hurries to see Calisto, which to Sempronio represents a new and unexpected movement in the old woman:

> O yo no veo bien, o aquélla es Celestina. ¡Válala el diablo, haldear que trahe! Parlando viene entre dientes.... el ánimo es forçado descobrillo por estas exteriores señales. ¿Quién jamás te vido hablar entre dientes por las calles y venir aguijando, como quien va a ganar beneficio? (V, 172)

Celestina is in such a hurry that she cannot stop to tell Sempronio what has occurred in Melibea's house. Her allegiance has shifted from Sempronio to Calisto because she knows that she no longer needs the servant's help to bring the affair to a prompt conclusion. On the contrary, any time spent speaking to him will only delay her payment from the *galán:* "Y assí que, mientra más tardasse, más caro me costasse" (V, 173). Sempronio is thrown off guard by Celestina's attitude because he is anxious to hear news about Melibea, but he soon discovers that Celestina has rethought his payment in the affair: "¿Partezilla, Celestina? Mal me parece esso que dizes" (V, 173).

Celestina has altered the clever but barely-profitable plan to extend the love affair and slowly strip away at Calisto's wealth, yet Sempronio agreed with the plan precisely because he thought that they would increase their profits the longer they maintained the fiction of this affair. Although Celestina tries to convince Sempronio otherwise, it is obvious that Sempronio has now lost all importance in her eyes. Celestina once stressed that they must work together, but when she speaks with Sempronio in act five, all of the references to work and benefit are in the first person, which shows that the profit in the affair will be entirely for her:

> El propóstio muda el sabio; el necio persevera. A nuevo negocio nuevo consejo se requiere. No pensé *yo*, hijo Sempronio, que assí *me* respondiera *mi* buena fortuna. De los discretos mensajeros es hazer lo que el tiempo quiere, assí que la calidad de lo hecho no puede encobrir tiempo dissimulado. Y más, que *yo* sé que tu amo, según lo que dél sentí, es liberal y algo antojadizo; más dará en un día de buenas nuevas que en ciento que ande pena[n]do y *yo* yendo y viniendo. (Our emphasis, V, 174)

Celestina tells Sempronio that time is telling the "discretos mensajeros" to change their plans, but this is one more mistaken interpretation of the passing of time in the work. She believes that time has forced her to change her plan, but she would have been better off if she had kept to their original bargain. More surprisingly, Celestina makes no effort to hide her change of plans from Sempronio. When they get to Calisto's house, Celestina and Sempronio hear that the *galán* cannot wait for her to arrive with news from Melibea. Sempronio wants Celestina to repeat the same lies they spoke outside of Calisto's door the first time they arrived in act one, but now she ignores Sempronio and emphasizes her own importance: "Calla, Sempronio, que aunque aya aventurado *mi* vida, más mereçe Calisto y su ruego y tuyo, y más mercedes espero *yo* dél" (our emphasis, V, 176).

When Celestina meets with Calisto, she sees that her plans seem to be working, although she only receives the promise of some new clothes from the young master. Pármeno cannot suffer her self-serving language any further because he knows that she is in a hurry to take advantage of a significant opportunity: "Y esta puta vieja querría en un día por tres passos desechar todo el pelo malo quanto en cinquenta años no ha podido medrar" (VI, 178). Although Pármeno later fools himself into believing that he should join Celestina in her plans to cheat Calisto, at this point he is still a capable observer of old woman's ways because he understands the other characters much better than he understands himself.

Sempronio begins to comprehend Celestina's plans in acts five and six, but he maintains his faith that things will work out in time.

Nevertheless, there is the threat of violence if they do not: "No tiene otra tacha sino ser codiciosa; pero déxala varde sus paredes, que después vardará las nuestras o en mal punto nos conoçió" (VI, 178). Sempronio knows that Celestina will not deal with them fairly, but he again suffers Celestina's lies because he is anxious to hear about Melibea. Celestina knows that Pármeno is still against her, but she doesn't realize that her greatest enemy is really Sempronio.

The next day, when Celestina returns to Calisto's house to tell him that Melibea wants to see him, the servants are no longer concerned about the love affair, but rather about the possibility of meeting a violent end if the rendezvous is a trick. Sempronio's cowardice is far stronger than his infatuation for the young woman, and for a poltroon like him the very speed with which she succumbed is warning enough. He has always wanted to have enough time to resolve things, and it is now evident that things are moving too quickly for his own good:

> SEMPRONIO. No sea ruydo hechizo, que nos quieren tomar a manos a todos; cata, madre, que assí se suelen dar las çaraças en pan embueltas, porque no las sienta el gusto.
> PÁRMENO. Nunca te oý dezir mejor cosa; mucha sospecha me pone el presto conceder de aquella señora. (XI, 252)

Since the two servants are afraid of how quickly the love affair is developing, Celestina would do well to slow things down for them and to reassure them that they will have time to save themselves. Unfortunately, the situation has become too large for her to handle. She has grown careless and is in such a hurry to leave the house with Calisto's gold chain that she pays little attention to Sempronio and Pármeno: "Señor, tú estás en lo cierto; vosotros cargados de sospechas vanas; yo he hecho todo lo que a mí era a cargo. Alegre te dexo; Dios te libre y aderece; pártome muy contenta. Si fuere menester para esto o para más, allí estoy muy aparejada a tu servicio" (XI, 253).

Virtually all of Celestina's words in Calisto's house in act eleven are directed at the young master, with only the short comment to the two servants that their concerns are "sospechas vanas" (XI, 253). While she does not pay attention to them, they cannot help but notice her desperation to leave the house and how much this final deal means to her:

SEMPRONIO. ¿De qué te rýes, por tu vida?
PÁRMENO. De la priessa que la vieja tiene por yrse; no vee la hora que haver despegado la cadena de casa; o puede creer que la tenga en su poder, ni que se la han dado de verdad; no se halla digna de tal don, tan poco como Calisto de Melibea.
SEMPRONIO. Qué quieres que haga una puta alcahueta, que sabe y entiende lo que nosotros [nos] callamos y suele hazer siete virgos por dos monedas, después de verse cargada de oro, sino ponerse en salvo con la possessión, con temor no se la tornen a tomar después que ha complido de su parte aquello para que era menester. ¡Pues guárdese del diablo, que sobre el partir no le saquemos el alma! (XI, 254)

Time now traps Celestina, Sempronio, and Pármeno. Celestina's astute and manipulative nature is neutralized by her advanced age and her desire to seize her final opportunity for material wealth. Pármeno thinks that he joins forces with Sempronio and Celestina in the nick of time, but he does not see that he brings about his own death when he eliminates the temporal difference between his past and present. Sempronio believes that time is a benign influence that will always keep him out of trouble, but he eventually understands that Celestina uses the speed of events to take advantage of the two servants.

When Pármeno and Sempronio return to the house in act twelve after the first visit to Pleberio's house, Sempronio's words reveal that he cannot allow Celestina any additional time with the gold necklace because she will use this time agains them: "[A]ntes que venga el día quiero yo yr a Celestina a cobrar mi parte de la cadena. Que es una puta vieja; no le quiero dar tiempo en que fabrique alguna ruyndad que nos escluya" (XII, 268). Time has run out for these three characters, and in their final minutes of life they will wish they had a few more moments to repent and confess their crimes.

Celestina always considered Pármeno to be an obstacle to her success, but until the end these two characters share a common problem in the way they relate the past and the present. Pármeno originally tries to deny the past and claim that he has severed all of his ties with his childhood, but he ends up affirming the essential equality of past and present when he returns to his previous dishonest life. Celestina also emphasizes the difference between her former standing in the city and her present penury, but she foolishly thinks that she can briefly turn back the clock and return to her former glory. Despite her verbal gifts, she is a tired and defeated woman who cannot manage one final affair, much less the affairs of the entire city. "Los días no [se] van embalde" (IV, 157), as Melibea observes, and the passing of time will not permit Celestina to recover her long-gone wealth. The return to the past destroys both characters, emphasizing time's inexorable and uncontrollable nature throughout the *Comedia*.

It is curious to note that Calisto barely feels the deaths of Celestina, Pármeno, and Sempronio because he only seems to regret his lost honor. Once he realizes the true nature of Celestina and his two servants, he understands that the tragedy was not so great because at some time or another they would have suffered the consequences of their actions: "Ellos eran sobrados y esforçados, agora o en otro tiempo de pagar havían" (XIII, 281). Despite his confusion, Calisto comprehends that time does not allow an escape for the guilty, although he never thinks to apply this understanding to his own life.

While Calisto's nature changes from an initial rush to an atemporal tranquility, Melibea's transformation works in the opposite direction. While she seems in control of herself the first day, by the second day she has lost her calm exterior and is burning with passion for Calisto. Celestina is readily aware of the young woman's altered state during their second meeting, and she brings out Melibea's feelings by deliberately playing with time. The young maiden wants an immediate resolution of her problem, but Celestina delays the conversations until Melibea cannot endure the wait any further: "Quanto más dilatas la cura, [Celestina,] tanto más *me* acrecientas y multiplicas la pena y passión.... ¡O como me muero con tu dilatar!" (X, 241, 242).

When Melibea opens up to Celestina, she is unable to hide her love for Calisto: "[L]o que abiertamente conosces en vano trabajo por te lo encobrir" (X, 245). Melibea has been hiding this love for a number of days, but now time becomes important to her and she is in a hurry to take advantage of every passing second. In this sense she has been transformed in time in the same way as Celestina because she demonstrates a tremendous force of acceleration once she knows that the stakes are much higher than she imagined. The only person who could have stopped Melibea's death was her mother, but once Alisa sees that there is a problem with Celestina's repeated visits, it is far too late to do anything about it. Alisa lectures Melibea about how evil Celestina is, but like every other character in the work, she is not well synchronized in time, as Lucrecia notes: "(Tarde acuerda nuestra ama)" (X, 248).

Celestina arranges a meeting between Calisto and Melibea for the second evening, and as midnight approaches Melibea is every bit as anxious as Calisto: "Mucho se tarda aquel cavallero que esperamos. ¿Qué crees tú o sospechas de su stada, Lucrecia?" (XIV, 283). Calisto is soon at her window to speak with her, and they will spend the next night together in Melibea's garden. Nevertheless, despite Calisto's death following their only evening together in the *Comedia*, Melibea does not express sorrow over their brief period of happiness. She is *desfasada* like every other character, and regrets that she she did not have more time to enjoy Calisto: "¡Oh la más de las tristes, triste, tan tarde alcançado el placer, tan presto venido el dolor! ... ¿Cómo no gozé más del gozo? ¿Cómo tove en tan poco la gloria que entre mis manos tove? Oh ingratos mortales, jamás conoscés vuestros bienes sino quando dellos carescéys" (XIX, 328).

Melibea has also been a victim of time because her love increased rather than cooled with the passing of the days: "Y en tal tiempo las fructuosas palabras, en lugar de amansar, acrescientan la seña" (XX, 332). During her final minutes on earth, Melibea is thinking of the time she has lost with Calisto, and her only consolation is that there are but a few moments remaining until she is reunited with the *galán*: "[A]lgún alivio siento en ver que tan presto seremos juntos yo y aquel mi querido y amado Calisto. ... no me atajen el camino por el qual en breve tiempo podré visitar en este día al que me visitó la passada noche" (XX, 331). The only way the characters can control time is by hurrying their own deaths, with the difference that it has been an inadvertent catastrophe for the other four main characters and a deliberate act for Melibea.

The complete inversion of time continues until the end of *Celestina*, when Pleberio wonders why he survives in old age while his young daughter has chosen to perish. He concludes that order has been disturbed by this death, and the novel ends in a temporal chaos with Pleberio's formerly tranquil life turned into a struggle to hurry time and meet his own death:

> Más dignos eran mis sesenta años de la sepultura, que tus veynte. Turbóse la orden del morir con la tristeza que te aquexava. O

> mis canas, salidas para aver pesar, mejor gozara de vosotras la tierra que de aquellos ruvios cabellos que presentes veo; fuertes días me sobran para bivir; quexarme he de la muerte; incusarla he su dilación, quanto tiempo me dexare solo después de ti. (XXI, 337)

With the affirmation of this disorder comes the realization that the characters lack the autonomy to control their own destinies in a disordered world. Although the characters attempt to hurry or slow down the progression of time throughout *Celestina,* a second form of time does not exist for them because they are invariably mistaken in the way they interpret time. As much as they try to take advantage of time or mitigate its passing, *Celestina*'s characters never present an alternative to an unavoidable and linear progression towards death and destruction. Time offers Calisto, Melibea, Celestina, Sempronio, and Pármeno a closed-end lease on life, and any other interpretation of time by these characters is no more than a tragic and fatal illusion.

IV

CALISTO AND THE IMPUTED PARODY OF COURTLY LOVE IN *CELESTINA*

Calisto is unquestionably the most problematical character for modern readers of Fernando de Rojas's *Celestina*. He is the protagonist of the best-known love story in the history of Spanish literature, yet this young hero suffers from love sickness, dishonest servants, self-doubt, dishonor, and apparent rejection from his beloved Melibea. After he overcomes these problems and consummates his love for Melibea during the third night of the *Comedia,* his misfortune continues when he falls to a horrible and senseless death outside of Pleberio's walls and dies without confession. More surprisingly, the *galán* Calisto is also upstaged by an ugly, old woman: for contemporary as well as modern readers, the *Comedia* and *Tragicomedia de Calisto y Melibea* are known simply as *Celestina,* even though the procuress's death in act twelve leaves the two lovers as the focus of the last half of the work.

Calisto's difficult and contradictory nature has created significant disagreement among modern scholars about how to interpret and categorize the young protagonist. María Rosa Lida de Malkiel (1962) analyzes Calisto's complex personality, and emphasizes the unusual relationship between his egoism and his dreamlike nature: "Calisto es el héroe egoísta o ensimismado en el sentido etimológico de esos términos: el soñador introspectivo absorbido en su yo" (348). Lida de Malkiel notes that Calisto lives at the margin of external reality and often finds himself in his bedroom on the border "entre sueño y vigilia" (348). Nothing exists for Calisto outside of his ever-changing imagination, and he invariably describes external events according to his exalted emotional state.

While the Latin humanistic comedy typically placed the protagonist in a well-defined social and family environment, Calisto follows the model of the "*Pamphilus,* con su protagonista enteramente aislado, mera personificación de una pasión individual, en contraste con la heroína, firmemente arraigada en el medio familiar y social" (351). With this undefined societal and personal environment, Calisto is free to immerse himself in his own words and imagination, which are profoundly influenced by other literary texts:

> El impulso a huir de la vida, esencial en todo soñador, coincide en Calisto con su afición literaria, pues la muerte por amores ha predominado como nunca en la lírica peninsular del siglo XV, de donde ha pasado a la novela sentimental. . . . El amor de Calisto está empapado de literatura. Los ecos de sus lecturas poéticas resuenan demasiado ruidosamente en sus palabras: el de Juan de Mena . . . en la salutación con que llega a los brazos de Melibea ("¡O angélico ymagen!") [XIV, 284], el de Pedro de la Costana al recibir su cordón [VI, 184], el de Diego de Quiñones al esperar su respuesta [VIII, 218]. El soliloquio del acto XIV destaca el seso cerebral de ese amor, del que Calisto debe convencerse a sí mismo con penoso razonamiento. (372, 373)

Peter N. Dunn (1975) notes how Calisto's solitary and unpredictable behavior makes it difficult to analyze and interpret him as a typical literary character. Unlike the protagonists of many earlier Latin comedies, Calisto does not actively participate in his love affair with Melibea, nor does he seek the assistance of clever and honest servants. Instead, Calisto plunges into the seclusion and despair of his darkened chamber and expresses his confused thoughts in a flowery language full of images of depression and death. The result is a singular and complicated character who at first does not seem to follow previous literary norms: "Thus the reader cannot tell from his first impression of the action and its tone what kind of character Calisto is or what kind of outcome to expect. He must not draw conclusions from antecedent literature but must read attentively" (108).

Dunn stresses that it is difficult to conclude that Calisto is a realistic character because we know so little about him. Although he is from a prominent family, Dunn repeats Lida's observation that we neither see Calisto's parents nor the young man's precise social position in the unnamed Spanish town. We only see Calisto in love, with the impetuousness and lack of judgment that this emotional state brings about:

> The action of *La Celestina,* seen from the perspective of Calisto, is his existence in love, the reorientation and subordination of his life to this passion. From the moment when the action begins, no other reality exists for Calisto. The form of the play mirrors the mind of Calisto: nothing from outside his situation of passion can exist within it.... Calisto's solitariness, his lack of contact with others, then, is less a matter of individualism in his personality than that of a symbolic reversal of what love should achieve. And the same may be said of the other aspects of his behavior. He is unable to separate dream and reality (acts XIII, XIV) or sacred and profane people and things. (110, 111-112)

Despite the complex and often contradictory portrait of Calisto that Lida and Dunn describe, some modern scholars believe that Calisto's problematical behavior can best be explained by *Celestina*'s parody of the courtly love tradition. As is well known, courtly love is a set of literary and behavioral conventions of courtesy and honor that evolved throughout medieval and Renaissance Europe. It is a form of woman-worship where the woman is elevated to an idealized, even divine plane, so the man renders service to the lady in order to prove himself worthy of her love and acceptance. While courtly love is conceived as an ennobling force that demonstrates the worth and virtue of the man, at the same time this love can increase its strength and desire and lead to love sickness, or *hereos*. June Hall Martin (1972) writes that the symptoms of this illness — most of which affect Calisto — include "paleness, sleeplessness, groaning, sighing, loss of appetite, palpitations of the heart, and even death" (11-12).[1]

For Alan Deyermond (1961), Calisto's form of speech in the book's opening scene represents a comic take-off on the courtly love manual *De Amore libri tres* of Andreas Capellanus. According to Deyermond, Calisto unsuccessfully relies on the *De Amore* as the textbook for his absurd attempt to woo Melibea, but his inappropriate use of the Capellanus model only serves to demonstrate the young man's foolishness:

---

[1] For a discussion of the conventions of courtly love, see Lewis (1-43), Martin (1-13), and Otis H. Green (1963: I, 73-122). For the concept of *hereos,* see Lowes, Green (1965: 26-27), and Couliano (19-23).

> Calisto's opening speech to Melibea is couched in flamboyant, exaggerated and – as it turns out – ludicrously unsuccessful terms. Melibea's ambiguous replies lead him on, and until the final and brutal disillusionment cuts him short, he becomes more and more deeply involved in his amatory rhetoric. We may well wonder why Calisto expected this approach to succeed; the answer, I suggest, is that this is the approach which his text-book told him to adopt. (218)

If the opening scene is a conscious yet unsuccessful use of the Capellanus text, as Deyermond believes, then Calisto's failure to conquer Melibea emphasizes his comic and parodic qualities. His ineffective reliance on Capellanus does not show him to be cultured or well-read, but rather a foolish young man who cannot make the transition from a medieval love manual to a Renaissance literary text.

June Hall Martin (1972) accepts Deyermond's conclusion that Calisto begins *Celestina* by mishandling Capellanus's *De Amore*, and she devotes a chapter of her book on courtly lovers to the idea of Calisto as a parody of this medieval form. Martin writes that,

> Careful examination of the *De Amore* reveals that Calisto is indeed misusing the textbook. He is in error from his very first words, as he begins bluntly: "En esto veo, Melibea, la grandeza de Dios." But Andreas has cautioned all lovers against such a direct approach.... From his first words... Calisto has insulted Melibea. He has approached her, according to Andreas, as men approach only their mistresses. (75)

While Martin asserts that Calisto is a parody of the courtly lover, or at least a failure as a courtly lover, much of her study demonstrates that Calisto has little in common with the conventions of courtesy and honor so important to courtly love:

> Calisto is clearly not born to be a courtly lover. He moves in a world of essentially bourgeois values and virtues. His world is so totally unlike that of Lancelot that the two may seem at first to have almost no relationship to one another (100).... His words lack the sincerity essential to the ideal courtly lover. His love lacks the power to ennoble him (101).... The reader... is continually aware of... the inherent foolishness of Calisto who has

pretension to being a courtly lover but who is continually being unmasked both by his servants and himself (122-23).... He is not a true courtly lover, despite his ... claims of servitude to his lady and his verbal obedience to the rules of love (126).

Since even Martin paints such a great contrast between Calisto's behavior and the tenets of courtly love, it is likely that *Celestina* does not represent a parody of the courtly lover at all. Martin believes that Calisto fails in his effort to be a courtly lover, but the great distance that she describes between Calisto's and Lancelot's worlds suggests that Calisto does not exist in a parodic text and that there is nothing mishandled in *Celestina*. According to Mikhail Bakhtin, a parody must be the recognizable image of the model text (1990: 51), but the relation between Calisto and the traditional courtly lover is so blurred that Martin has trouble deciding if or where the parody exists: "Calisto's baseness, glossed over by a thin layer of courtly learning, leads one to the conclusion that it is perhaps in this enormous gap between what Calisto is and what he pretends to be that the parody lies.... What Rojas is attacking is not so much the true courtly lover, but the false – he who pretends to be what he is not" (112-13).

Dorothy Severin (1989) ignores the possible defects in Martin's study of Calisto and concludes that "Calisto is a parodic courtly lover, as June Hall Martin has shown" (23). Unlike Dunn, Severin believes that Calisto's relation to previous texts is evident from the work's very first scene; his parodic nature is so obvious that contemporary listeners and readers would have immediately understood the young man's comic ridiculousness: "Even if the reader was unaware of the misuse of Andreas Capellanus in Calisto's approach, Melibea's sarcastic reaction was the clue: 'Pues, ¡aún más ygual galardón te daré yo, si perseveras!'" (24).

Severin thinks that the text's parodic nature underlines *Celestina*'s comic aspects, which revolve around the work's amusingly foolish protagonist. Learned fifteenth- and sixteenth-century readers would have clearly seen the caricature of the courtly lover represented by Leriano in Diego de San Pedro's *Cárcel de amor*.[2] Never-

---

[2] María Eugenia Lacarra (1989), who agrees with Deyermond, Severin, and Martin, writes that "En el acto I ... se establece la parodia del amor cortesano representado por el género sentimental y más concretamente por el que desarrollan

theless, Severin is seemingly surprised that most scholars have taken so long to understand *Celestina's* parodic quality: "[A]stoundingly enough, modern critics overlooked this obvious point until the last few years... As recent criticism has pointed out, the primitive author and Rojas both develop and emphasize the parody repeatedly throughout the work" (25).

According to Severin, in act one Calisto is no more than "a love-besotted nitwit" who is "an unworthy lover for a nice girl with a slightly sharp tongue" (25). Rojas develops his protagonist in the continuation of the work, but he "could not... change Calisto, whose parodic character was too well established [in the *Auto*] to be metamorphosed" (26). Any development in Calisto only serves to make "Melibea's suicide more plausible and more tragic" (26) because it would be illogical for her to commit suicide over the "madman and fool" (25) that Severin describes. Despite this overwhelming criticism of Calisto, Severin allows the *galán* some minor development in the latter part of the *Comedia*, and slightly more so in the *Tragicomedia*:

> However, after the deaths of both of his servants and the bawd Celestina in Act XII, and after the first night of love in the garden, Calisto does seem to evolve from mere parody to a more interesting and serious figure in whom imagination is of paramount importance. In Act XIV he relives his first night of love in his imagination: "Pero tú, dulce ymaginación, tú que puedes me acorre; trae a mi fantasía la presencia angélica de aquella ymagen luziente; buelve a mis oýdos el suave son de sus palabras..." [XIV, 292].... Rojas seems to give Calisto a second chance in the additional acts [of the *Tragicomedia*] to evolve away from mere parody, although the result is often cowardly and despicable. (27-28)

Severin's argument perhaps falters when she concludes that Calisto is a feeble, parodic character who changes and develops in the

---

los personajes principales de *Cárcel de amor*, como señala Severin. La retórica del diálogo inicial responde al lenguaje del código amoroso cortesano, propio tanto de la ficción sentimental como de la poesía lírica amorosa. Sin embargo, ya en ese primer diálogo entre Calisto y Melibea existen elementos que nos ponen sobre aviso de la distorsión a que se somete este lenguaje cortesano.... Estoy de acuerdo con Deyermond sobre la influencia de *De amore* de Andreas Capellanus en esta primera escena y con su conclusión de que Calisto se muestra como un mal discípulo" (13-14).

Tragicomedia into "a more interesting and serious figure in whom imagination is of paramount importance" (28). Lida de Malkiel has emphasized the importance of Calisto's dreamlike and imaginative nature, so Severin's approach may well gloss over the fundamental part of Calisto's personality. Moreover, as we have shown in previous chapters of this study, Calisto's imagination begins to develop in the dreamworld vision of the primitive *Celestina*'s opening scene, and not in act fourteen of the *Tragicomedia*. If this invented world is indeed proof of Calisto's creativity and his depth of character, then we must conclude that Calisto has shown these qualities from the very beginning of the text and thus reject the idea of Calisto as a weak and awkward caricature of Leriano.³

More importantly, the very notion of Calisto as a parody of the courtly lover in Deyermond, Martin, and Severin rests entirely on their unique reading of *Celestina*'s first scene. According to these three critics, the bumbling Calisto declares his love to Melibea in scene one because he misunderstands the linguistic and behavioral codes of courtly love, and he continues his foolish speech to the young woman because he is not astute enough to perceive the cruel irony of Melibea's ambiguous response. Nevertheless, the idea of Calisto's dream strongly suggests that Calisto's problem in the anonymous *Auto* is not a misunderstanding or a misuse of the *De Amore* at all, but on the contrary a close and accurate reading of the Capellanus text.

There is an important explanation of the nature of Calisto's opening dream in the section of the *De Amore* entitled "A Nobleman Addresses a Noblewoman." Since this part of the *De Amore* shows how a man of high birth should speak to a woman of similar social standing, it is appropriate to describe the relationship between Calisto and Melibea in *Celestina*. According to Capellanus, the most important symptom of the nobleman's love melancholy is the constant mental presence of his beloved. He wants to observe her physically, but since this is not always possible he is forced to recall her visual image, as he tells her in this section of the *De Amore:*

---

³ It is likely that the scene that Severin cites from act fourteen is in reality a joyous reprise of the *Auto*'s opening scene. Calisto calls upon his imagination to once again "trae[r] a [su] fantasía la presencia angélica de aquella ymagen luziente" (XIV, 292), which is the same thing that occured in the first scene, as noted in the book's *Argumento*: "[A] la presencia de Calisto se presentó la deseada Melibea" (83).

> Though I appear before your eyes rarely in the flesh, in heart and mind I am never out of your presence. My thoughts which dwell continually on you often plant me in your company, causing me perpetually to gaze with the eyes of the heart on that treasure on which my attention lingers, and bringing me both pains and abundant consolation. (97)

While the nobleman always maintains his lady's image in his thoughts, Capellanus believes that her vision can control much more than his wakeful imagination. The overpowering strength of love sickness is such that the woman's image takes over the world of the young man's dreams, so he will end up seeing her in his nighttime as well as daytime fantasy. The nobleman explains his infatuation to the noblewoman by telling her that,

> [W]hen I cannot see you physically ... all the surrounding elements begin to beset me, and different kinds of pains to bruise me. I can rejoice in no consolation, save in the deceiving portrayal brought to me by drowsy slumber as I sleep. But though Sleep sometimes cheats me with such unreal bounty, I still offer feeling thanks to him for having sought to beguile me with such sweet and noble deception. (97, 99)

Calisto's dream of Melibea during the first morning of *Celestina* is therefore the precise lovesick behavior that the *De Amore* tells us to expect from a young man of Calisto's social position. Melibea appears in act one only as a "deceiving portrayal brought to [Calisto] by drowsy slumber" (99), although unfortunately this vision still continues to fool readers almost five centuries later. We may note that Lida de Malkiel's astute observation that Calisto lives between "sueño y vigilia" (340) corresponds directly to the Capellanus text, since dreams are a fundamental part of contemporary theories of love sickness.

The introduction to the *De Amore* provides further information about the nature of Calisto's fantasy of Melibea. According to Capellanus, a young man's passion is created entirely inside of his mind after he sees a beautiful woman, and this feeling of overpowering love grows until the young man finds himself suffering from the incessant and imaginative contemplation of the woman's physical attributes. Calisto's fantastic vision of Melibea in scene one – what the *De Amore* calls "such sweet and noble deception" (99) –

is simply a typical result of love melancholy that occurs after the woman's image invades the man's body through his eyes. Capellanus writes that,

> I can demonstrate by a clear argument that the feeling of love is inborn.... [I]t arises not from any action, but solely from the thought formed by the mind as a result of the thing seen. When a man sees a girl ripe for love and fashioned to his liking, he at once begins to desire her inwardly, and whenever subsequently he thinks about her, he burns with love for her more each time, until then he reaches the stage of detailed reflexion. (35)

The sensual, limitless wonder of love melancholy permeates Calisto's speech throughout the first scene, but his uncontrolled desires remain unfulfilled because Melibea's image unexpectedly rejects his advances. Despite the "pensamientos tristes" that plague Calisto following this rejection (I, 89), the introduction to the *De Amore* prescribes the same solution to this problem that we find in the first act of *Celestina*. Capellanus reveals that a young man who suffers from the detailed reflection of his beloved should find a helper and a go-between to assist him, so the *De Amore* indicates that Calisto – by seeking the aid of Sempronio and Celestina – follows rather than caricatures the medieval model:

> Now when he attains this stage of detailed reflexion, his love cannot keep control over its reins, but at once advances to action. Immediately he is at pains to enrol a helper and to find a go-between. He begins to think how he can win her favour, and to contrive a place and time affording opportunity to converse. He thinks a mere hour an interminable year, because no fulfilment can come quickly enough to a longing heart.... Any casual meditation is not enough to cause love; the thoughts must be out of control, for a controlled thought does not usually recur to the mind, and so love cannot arise from it. (35)

This passage describes the first scenes of *Celestina* very accurately. Calisto awakens the first morning of act one suffering from uncontrolled thoughts of his beloved Melibea. His imagination briefly fooled him into believing that he had discovered a "tan conveniente lugar" to speak with the young woman (I, 86) – what Capellanus calls a "place and time affording opportunity to converse" with her (35) – but his foul mood upon awakening reflects his disappointment at finding himself alone in his chamber. Calisto then enlists the help of his servant Sempronio, and he agrees to hire Celestina as a go-between once Sempronio mentions her name. Soon afterwards, since "no fulfilment can come quickly enough to a longing heart" (35), Calisto pleads for divine intervention to speed and guide Sempronio on his vital mission to Celestina's house.

Since Calisto's behavior fits the traditional lovesick young man described by Capellanus, it is unsurprising that Rojas and later Renaissance authors recognized the *galán*'s opening dream and included it in their own Celestinesque works. Rojas's continuation of *Celestina* clearly suggests that he understood that Calisto suffered from recurring dreams about Melibea, which would confirm the strong relationship between the *galán*'s behavior and the symptoms of love melancholy described in the *De Amore*. In act six, for example, during the work's first evening, Celestina returns to Calisto's house with news from Melibea. Calisto immediately asks her to accompany him to his chamber so that he can hear the episode in his bed, so he ends up listening to his own love story in the same place that he has previously imagined it in his dreams. Calisto hangs on Celestina's every word until the old woman tells him that Melibea has sent him her *cordón* in order to cure his illness. The *galán* then asks for the cordon and then reveals that he has been dreaming about Melibea every evening:

> CALISTO. Gozará mi lastimado coraçón, aquel que nunca recibió momento de plazer después que aquella señora conoció. Todos los sentidos le llagaron; todos acorrieron a él con su esportillas de trabajo; cada uno le lastimó quanto más pudo: los ojos en vella, los oýdos en oýlla, las manos en tocalla.
> CELESTINA. ¿Qué [sic] la has tocado, dizes? Mucho me espantas.
> CALISTO. Entre sueños, digo.
> CELESTINA. ¿En sueños?
> CALISTO. En sueños la veo tantas noche que temo no me acontezca como a Alcibíades [o a Sócrates]. . . .
> CELESTINA. Assaz tienes pena, pues quando los otros reposan en sus camas, preparas tú el trabajo para sofrir otro día. . . .
> CALISTO. ¡[O] bienaventurado cordón. . . . Dezíme si os hallastes presentes en la desconsolada respuesta de aquella a quien vosotros servís y yo adoro, y por más que trabajo noches y días, no me vale ni aprovecha. (VI, 185-86)

Calisto thus reveals during *Celestina*'s first evening that he has spent the previous nights dreaming about Melibea, and that he has seen her and heard her words in his nighttime imagination. Rojas would have included this passage in act six because he realized that act one begins in Calisto's imagination, and that it was likely that the *galán* experienced similar fantasies during the previous evenings. More importantly, Calisto's opening dream indicates that the figure of Melibea appears in the first act only in the form of phantasy, so instead of exerting mastery over the inept and parodic Calisto, the young woman's very existence in the *Auto* depends on the *galán*'s imagination and linguistic creativity. Calisto is not dominated by Melibea's sharp tongue or sarcastic treatment, but instead by his own deteriorating mental and physical condition as a result of his passionate love for the young woman. The complicated and confusing language of the opening scene does not represent a stylized linguistic game of ignorance and sarcasm, but rather the *antiguo auctor*'s deliberate attempt to reproduce the irrational and uncontrolled dreams of a young man suffering from love melancholy.

Since Calisto's ailment closely follows the explanation of love melancholy found in Capellanus and other Medieval and Renaissance *tratadistas*,[4] it seems clear that the young protagonist has not mishandled the *De Amore* at all. On the contrary, by emphasizing *Celestina*'s supposedly parodic nature, Deyermond, Martin, Lacarra, and Severin have seriously distorted Calisto's character by failing to consider Lida de Malkiel's observations about the importance of the *galán*'s creative use of borrowed texts. According to Bakhtin, the prose writer uses different forms of speech in the creation of the modern novel. This multiplicity of linguistic and literary forms establishes the basis of the novel, including a dialogic work like *Celestina*:

---

[4] The *galán*'s continuous contemplation of his beloved in his imagination is a common element in many Medieval and Renaissance treatises on love melancholy. Arnaldus de Vilanova mentions the *cogitationem in ea frequentius* (Lowes 496), Bernardus Gordonius the *continua meditatione* (Lowes 499), Constantino the *afflictione cogitationum* (Lowes 515), while Capellanus refers to the *immoderata cogitatione* (32).

For a more complete study of the origins and the nature of Calisto's love sickness, see my "El mal de amores de Calisto y el diagnóstico de Eras y Crato, médicos." For love melancholy in the Spanish Golden Age, see Soufas (1990).

> Thus even where there is no comic element, no parody, no irony and so forth, where there is no narrator, no posited author or narrating character, speech diversity and language stratification still serve as the basis for style in the novel. Even in those places where the author's voice seems at first glance to be unitary and consistent, direct and unmediatedly intentional, beneath that smooth single-languaged surface we can nevertheless uncover prose's three-dimensionality, its profound speech diversity, which enters the project of style and is its determining factor. (1990: 315)

The use of others' words or the refraction of previous literary styles does not mean that the author is automatically writing a parody of existing works. Instead, the author consciously introduces borrowed speech into his text for his own artistic purposes.[5] Rather than parody Leriano, the polyglot Calisto mimics the linguistic style and the conventions of amorous literature; he quotes and distorts classical authors and he sings absurd *romances amorosos;* he laughs, cries, and yells; and often he also expresses himself in popular speech. He is a complex yet confusing multi-faceted character, and certainly not a simplistic, constrained caricature of the courtly lover. Significantly, the best example of Calisto's linguistic creativity is his flawless domination of literary amorous discourse in acts twelve and nineteen, although this is the form of speech that he supposedly mishandles.

While Calisto is not a traditional courtly lover, he maintains some courtly traditions. He considers himself subservient to Melibea, whom he deifies repeatedly, and of course he suffers many of the symptoms of love sickness. Nevertheless, Calisto does not believe love to be an ennobling, virtuous force. Calisto's interests lie in the physical plane because he is neither parodic nor constrained by medieval literary canons. Calisto establishes dialogic contact with previous texts, but with the expressed intention of exceeding the

---

[5] While *Celestina* is not precisely a modern novel, Bakhtin's description of the single-voice novel as a form of closet drama reveals that *Celestina* instead fits under Bahktin's characterization of the polyglot text: "The novel, when torn out of authentic linguistic speech diversity, emerges in most cases as a 'closet drama,' with detailed, fully developed and 'artistically worked out' stage directions (it is, of course, bad drama). In such a novel, divested of its language diversity, authorial language inevitably ends up in the awkward and absurd position of the language of stage directions in plays" (1990: 327).

scope of the now outmoded model. He therefore follows the formulaic, medieval description of Melibea's physical and moral attributes in act one (I, 100-01), but he also laments his inability to describe "lo occulto" (I, 100), an area that cannot be copied because it does not exist in previous literary works. Calisto continually attempts to create a new and dynamic literary space for his love affair, which is the complete opposite of the limited artistic function of a parodic character.[6]

Since much of the confusion on Calisto's supposedly parodic nature comes from a mistaken interpretation of scene one, it is useful to reexamine the opening conversation between Calisto and Melibea in order to develop a different approach to the text. Calisto speaks only four brief sentences to Melibea in the first scene, along with one longer statement. The confusion doubtlessly comes from the longer statement, which begins as follows:

> En dar poder a natura que de tan perfecta hermosura te dotasse, y hazer a mí, inmérito, tanta merced que verte alcançasse, y en tan conveniente lugar, que mi secreto dolor manifestarte pudiesse. Sin duda, incomparablemente es mayor tal galardón que el servicio, sacrificio, devoción y obras pías que por este lugar alcançar yo tengo a Dios offrecido [ni otro poder mi voluntad humana puede cumplir]. (I, 86)

At first glance, Calisto may appear to recite from traditional amorous literature. He speaks of Melibea's perfect beauty, and declares that he is unworthy of such a prize. What is more, he mentions "el servicio, sacrificio, devoción y obras pías que por este lugar alcançar tengo a Dios offrecido" (I, 86), reflecting the service and sacrifice of the courtly lover. Yet the key to understanding the

---

[6] The dialogical relationship that Calisto experiences between the symptoms of heroical love and amorous literature was later documented in Robert Burton's *The Anatomy of Melancholy* (1621), the most extensive treatment of this malady in English. In her study of Burton's work, Ruth A. Fox writes: "And so the final symptom of love melancholy: as fictions make men love, men in love make fictions" (156). According to Burton, "[A]bove all the other symptoms of love . . . if once they be in love, they turn to their ability, rhymers, ballad-makers and poets. For as Plutarch saith, 'They will be witnesses and trumpeters of their paramours' good parts, bedecking them with verses and commendatory songs'" (III.3.2.3: 578). Burton repeatedly cites Calisto as a typical example of love melancholy (III.2.3; 557, 558, 560, 568).

For Calisto as *trobador*, see *Celestina* (I, 91; VIII, 218-19; and XIII, 276).

passage is the consciously repeated reference to the place where the scene takes place: the "tan conveniente lugar" and "este lugar" (I, 86). This convenient place is not a location similar to the medieval garden of the *Roman de la Rose*,[7] but rather Calisto's own bedroom. It would be difficult to imagine a more convenient place for a young couple than the young man's chamber, so from the very beginning of the *Auto* we see that *Celestina* will create its own kind of *locus amoenus*.

Rojas's continuation of the text affirms and emphasizes the importance of Calisto as a character who lives in a world made up of borrowed texts and ideas. Throughout Rojas's work, Calisto stages a literary performance with his own bedroom as the theater and his bed at center stage. The *galán* receives Celestina downstairs when she comes to the house for the first time in act one, but at the beginning of the second act Sempronio gets Calisto back into his chamber, which represents his natural, dreamlike habitat. Calisto's fundamental problem is his failure to organize his imagination in a coherent fashion, which is the essence of his confusion in the opening scene. Instead of imagining a happy ending to the dream about Melibea, for example, he has chaotic thoughts that do not lead to a successful conclusion to his love. Calisto has already indicated his inability to fully describe Melibea in the first act, but in act two of Rojas's continuation he tells Sempronio that his love melancholy prevents him from speaking adequately to Celestina as well:

> Sabido eres; fiel te siento; por buen criado te tengo; haz de manera que en sólo verte ella a ti, juzgue la pena que a mí queda y fuego que me atormenta, cuyo ardor me causó no poder mostrarle la tercia parte desta mi secreta enfermedad, según tiene mi lengua y sentido ocupados y consumidos. Tú, como hombre libre de tal passión, hablarla has a rienda suelta. (II, 131-132)

Calisto's comments may seem ludicrous at first to the modern reader, but even Calisto recognizes them to be the result of his excessive passion. The idea of a supposedly parodic character is further undermined by this self-conscious admission, which again demonstrates that he is no ignorant fool. Sempronio is also fully

---

[7] See Martin (80-93).

aware of Calisto's malady by act two, as well as of Calisto's customary fantastic imagination:

> ¿Mas cómo yré?, que en viéndote solo, dizes desvaríos de hombre sin seso, sospirando, gemiendo, maltrobando, holgando con lo escuro, desseando soledad, buscando nuevos modos de pensativo tormento, donde, si perseveras, o de muerto o loco no podrás escapar, si siempre no te acompaña quien... sepa buscar todo género de dulce passatiempo para no dexar trasponer tu pensamiento en aquellos crueles desvíos que recebiste de aquella señora en el primer trance de tus amores. (II, 132)

Calisto's nature is to search for these "nuevos modos de pensativo tormento" because his *devaneos* do not follow any form of reasoned discourse. Sempronio wants to separate Calisto from his imagination because the *galán* is literally *sin seso,* but Calisto wants to act this way because his behavior is shaped entirely by texts that he has read:

> ¿Cómo, simple, no sabes que alivia la pena llorar la causa? ¿Quánto es dulce a los tristes quexar su passión? ¿Quánto descanso traen consigo los quebrantados sospiros? ¿Quánto relievan y disminuyen los lagrimosos gemidos el dolor? Quantos scrivieron consuelos no dizen otra cosa. (II, 132)

Calisto reveals that he is merely following the instruction in these texts, but Sempronio argues that Calisto should better choose how to interpret these works: "Lee más adelante. Buelve la hoja" (II, 133). Yet while they disagree on the correct reading of previous texts, they both seem to accept that the *galán* will live his life as dramatic and dreamlike literature.

Celestina returns to Calisto's house in the sixth act, but her main concern is to impress Calisto with the importance of her work so that he will give her more money for her effort. Celestina, the manipulator of earthy speech, now speaks in uselessly formal discourse: "O mi señor Calisto, ¿y aquí estás? O mi nuevo amador de la muy hermosa Melibea, y con mucha razón, ¿con qué pagarás a la vieja que hoy ha puesto su vida al tablero por tu servicio? ¿Quál mujer jamás se vido en tan estrecha afrenta como yo?" (VI, 176-77). As is often the case in *Celestina,* the use of formal speech does not help the speaker because Calisto is interested only in his own love story, and not in Celestina's reporting of her financial troubles: "Madre mía, o abrevia tu razón, o toma esta spada y mátame" (VI, 177).

While the other characters often serve as literary critics to Calisto's borrowed literary speech, on this occasion he is able to turn the tables on Celestina because she is using a language that is inappropriate for a character from the lower rungs of society. Formal discourse in *Celestina* works only between Calisto and Melibea because they have the literary and social backgrounds appropriate for this form of expression. Nevertheless, once Celestina begins to talk about Melibea in normal speech, Calisto is again captivated by her rhetoric, so he must return to his natural habitat in order to fully enjoy the story: "Ya me reposa el coraçón; ya descansa mi pensamiento;... ya tengo alegría. Subamos, si mandas, arriba. En mi cámara me dirás por estenso lo que aquí he sabido en suma" (VI, 180).

Calisto has not been able to see Melibea since their chance meeting some days before, so he has only two alternatives if he wants to immerse himself in his love for the young woman. First, he can enjoy Melibea vicariously through Celestina's narration:

> CELESTINA. Recebí, señor, tanta alteración de plazer que qualquiera que me viera me lo conosciera en el rostro.
> CALISTO. Agora la recibo yo, quanto más quien ante sí contemplava tal ymagen. (VI, 181-82)

Second, Calisto can also create his own fictional reality in his dreamworld. Both alternatives produce the same pleasure and have the same physical location in his bedroom, but the dreams allow Calisto physical possibilities that even Celestina has not yet imagined: "[Entre sueños] [t]odos los sentidos le llagaron; todos acorrieron a él con su esportillas de trabajo; cada uno le lastimó quanto más pudo: los ojos en vella, los oýdos en oýlla, las manos en tocalla" (VI, 185).

This nighttime world full of ornate and exaggerated speech makes Calisto look ridiculous to Celestina and the servants, but his ability to absorb and refract others' words is precisely what later assures his success with Melibea. During the *Auto*'s second evening, Calisto visits the young woman outside of her window, but there is no longer any hint of absurd language from the young lover. Despite Calisto's unusual comportment before this encounter, Baldassare Castiglione's *Il libro del Cortegiano* explains that it is normal for a young man in the midst of a sensual passion to change his behavior in the presence of his beloved. Although Castiglione notes that the *inamorati* feel nothing but "affani, tormenti, dolori, stenti, [e] fatiche" (LII, 332), their souls feel immediate relief when they are finally reunited with their beloved: "[L]'anima ... quasi diventa furiosa, fin che quella cara belleza se le appresenta un'altra volta; ed allor sùbito s'acqueta e respira ed a quella tutta intenta si nutrisce di cibo dulcissimo, né mai da così suave spettacolo partir vorria" (LXVI, 344).

Calisto has been practicing for his rendezvous with Melibea in his imagination for days, and his assignation with the young woman allows him to return to the darkened world that he dominates completely. When Melibea asks, "Ce, señor, ¿cómo es tu nombre? ¿Quién es el que te mandó aý venir?" (XII, 259), Calisto does not respond with a simple statement as Sempronio or Pármeno would do. Instead, he answers with the flowery literary language that has become his trademark:

> Es la que tiene mereçimiento de mandar a todo el mundo, la que dignamente servir yo no merezco. No tema tu merced de se descobrir a este cativo de su gentileza, que el dulce sonido de tu habla que jamás de mis oýdos se cae, me certifica ser tú mi señora Melibea. Yo soy tu siervo Calisto. (XII, 259-60)

Melibea goes through a perfunctory defense of her honor, but Calisto responds with an impassioned lament that convinces her of his sincerity and the depth of his love. Instead of creating a parodic scene, Calisto plays the role of the literary lover to perfection as he shifts his nighttime performance from his bedroom to Melibea's window. He reveals himself a captive of his lady's love and admits that he is unworthy of her, as the literary model demands. Calisto thus demonstrates that he is no love-besotted nitwit, but rather a sincere and cultured young man whom Melibea accepts as her ideal lover in their nighttime world:

> Cessen, señor mío, tus verdaderas querellas, que ni mi coraçón basta para las sofrir, ni mis ojos para lo dissimular. Tú lloras de tristeza juzgándome cruel; yo lloro de plazer viéndote tan fiel. ¡O

> mi señor y mi bien todo, quánto más alegre me fuera poder veer tu haz que oýr tu boz! Pero pues no se puede al presente más hazer, toma la firma y sello de las razones que te embié scritas en la lengua de aquella solícita mensajera. Todo lo que te dixo confirmo; todo he por bueno; limpia, señor, tus ojos; ordena de mí a tu voluntad. (XII, 260-61)

Since she cannot see him, Calisto has convinced Melibea exclusively with the emotional sincerity of his words, which are made up of the borrowed speech that he uses in the love story that he now acts out. Although the visual contact with the beloved is essential for Castiglione, for Rojas the two lovers' verbal contact is paramount.[8] Calisto's imaginary literary text finally meets its proper context in Melibea's presence, and the language flows naturally between them in a way that could never occur between Calisto and any of the other characters in the book. Calisto's and Melibea's superior education and social position are revealed by their dialogic contact and their use of the same form of amorous discourse. Their linguistic equality demonstrates that Melibea is not superior to Calisto in any way; they share the same language and the same feelings, and so they employ the same form of expression for their love.

Calisto agrees to see Melibea the following evening in her garden, and in this way makes the final transition from the interior, nighttime world of his bedroom to the expansive nighttime world outside of Melibea's house. After seeing Melibea again, he does not suffer from fitful dreams during the work's second evening because the memory of his meeting with Melibea has taken the place of the imaginary conversations that Calisto had previously created: "¡Oh cómo he dormido tan a mi plazer después de aquel açucarado rato, después de aquel angélico razonamiento!" (XIII, 275). Calisto even wonders whether the whole conversation was not dream because the real Melibea has displaced the invented Melibea that used to dominate his thoughts and imagination.

The evening in the garden in act fourteen completes the *Comedia*'s cycle that began in Calisto's chamber in the work's first scene. Calisto has often dreamed of effortlessly touching Melibea, but now

---

[8] In the interpolated acts of the *Tragicomedia,* Lucrecia suggests in a *romance* that the lovers experience visual joy even in the darkness: "Alegre es la fuente clara / a quien con gran sed la vea, / mas muy dulce es la cara / de Calisto a Melibea. / Pues aunque más noche sea / con su vista gozará" (XIX, 321).

that he has her close by he must rely on his literary speech to convince her to succumb to his carnal desires:

> Señora, pues por conseguir esta merced toda mi vida he gastado, ¿qué sería, quando me la diessen, desechalla?.... No me pides tal covardía; no es hazer tal cosa de ninguno que hombre sea, mayormente amando como yo, nadando por este huego de tu desseo toda mi vida. ¿No quieres que me arrime al dulce puerto a descansar de mis passados trabajos? (XIV, 284-85)

Melibea puts up token resistance to Calisto's advances, but she cannot keep Calisto on an entirely verbal level, even though she clearly enjoys his words of love: "Por mi vida, que aunque hable tu lengua quanto quisiere, no abren las manos quanto pueden" (XIV, 285).

After his evening in Melibea's garden during the *Comedia*'s final day, Calisto falls alone into the darkness and dies in the same shadowy nighttime world that he lived in. Calisto has taken his amorous dreams about Melibea to the sensual and material plane of physical love, but even his extensive imagination could not have anticipated the unfortunate and tragic end to his love affair. While Calisto is an often absurd and comic character before he is reunited with Melibea in act twelve, he is a far more complicated figure than some modern critics have realized. His most important trait is his use of existing literary languages, although these forms of expression find their ideal context only in the darkness of his chamber and in the nighttime world outside outside of Melibea's house. His cultured speech makes him an anomaly for Celestina and his servants, but it also makes him the ideal literary lover for Melibea. Calisto's moments of apparent ridiculousness and exaggerated discourse become his preparation for the two meetings with the young woman in the *Comedia*, encounters where the *galán*'s literary language reveals its poetic quality and his complex and multi-layered use of others' words.

V

MELIBEA'S SWIFT SURRENDER: CHARACTERIZATION
AND SELF-REALIZATION IN *CELESTINA*

Although Calisto has proven to be the most enigmatic of *Celestina*'s main characters, Melibea has also perplexed generations of Fernando de Rojas's readers. The young woman's sensual desires and independence of spirit have startled critics since the beginning of the sixteenth century because this behavior challenges the reader's expectations of how a young woman in Renaissance Spain should act. Only three decades after the publication of *Celestina*, Juan de Valdés writes in *El diálogo de la lengua* that Rojas presents most of the characters in a realistic fashion, but that Melibea demonstrates certain temporal and psychological contradictions: "La [persona] de Celestina stá a mi ver perfetíssima en todo quanto pertenece a una fina alcahueta, y las de Sempronio y Pármeno; la de Calisto no stá mal y la de Melibea pudiera estar mejor . . . [porque] se dexa muy presto vencer, no solamente a amar, pero a gozar del deshonesto fruto del amor" (175). Although many of *Celestina*'s first readers enjoyed Calisto's and Melibea's love affair, Valdés concludes that Melibea's swift surrender – what he calls her *presto vencer* – does not demonstrate the decorum expected of a young woman of high birth and proper sentiments. This judgment reveals not only the perspective of a religious writer who must confront Melibea's moral transgressions, but also Valdés's vision of a character whose behavior violates the literary and social mores of her age.

Marcelino Menéndez Pelayo considers that Valdés's criticism of Melibea is valid but somewhat harsh. Don Marcelino finds dramatic motives to explain Melibea's sudden fall from grace, and justifies the unexpected change in the young woman through Celestina's diabolic and overpowering influence:

> Grave reparo puso al carácter de Melibea Juan de Valdés, y. . . . ciertamente que es así, pero no sin circunstancias, unas muy humanas y otras diabólicas, que aceleren su caída y la expliquen dentro de la verosimilitud dramática. La misma Melibea ha contestado anticipadamente a su crítico: ["(M)i amor fue con justa causa. Requerida y rogada, cativada de su merecimiento, aquexada por tan astuta maestra como Celestina, servida de muy peligrosas visitaciones, antes que concediesse por entero en su amor" (XVI, 305)]. Mucho más rápido procede el enamoramiento de Julieta, aunque no sea deshonesto el fruto de su amor ni trabajen por él los espíritus del Averno. (152)

For Valdés and Menéndez Pelayo, Melibea's lapse is a moral fault that affects the way they visualize and interpret her as a literary character. When Menéndez Pelayo writes that, "Grave reparo puso al carácter de Melibea Juan de Valdés," don Marcelino is not simply trying to explain the dramatic change in Melibea. Menéndez Pelayo also attempts to uphold her literary and moral reputation while affirming the temporal realism of Rojas's work. When he stresses Melibea's susceptibility to Celestina's cunning manipulation, don Marcelino asserts that the young woman is not entirely to blame for her fall, although he notes the strength and uncontrolled power of her sensual passion.

Modern critics have observed the strong relationship between the work's temporal development and the realism of Fernando de Rojas's characterization of Melibea. As we have noted, María Rosa Lida de Malkiel believes that the text requires more time between Melibea's rejection of Calisto's advances during their first meeting at the beginning of the work, and the young woman's prompt acceptance of Calisto's love in acts ten and twelve. Lida therefore shares some of the same concerns about Melibea's *presto vencer* that Juan de Valdés expressed in the sixteenth century, although within a literary rather than a moral sphere: "La insistencia con que se alude a este compás de espera apunta al móvil del curioso procedimiento: hacer verosímil, dentro de su carácter, la entrega de Melibea, que resultaría inconcebible si, rechazando airadamente a Calisto a la mañana del primer día, se le rinde ciega a la tarde del día siguiente" (177). Lida de Malkiel attempts to resolve the problem of *Celestina*'s psychological and temporal realism by affirming that a certain amount of time must have passed between the first and second scenes of act one. The text permits actions that are "simultáneas sin ser verosímilmente coextensivas en el tiempo" (181), so the temporal separation between scenes one and two is consistent with the work's unorthodox time flow.

P. E. Russell (1978) has also studied the sudden change in Melibea's attitude towards Calisto, and concludes that it can only be the result of a *philocaptio,* a magic spell that unconsciously forces a person to love another. Like Menéndez Pelayo, Russell believes that there are good reasons for Melibea's fall, and that the young woman has shown remarkable resistance to Celestina's overpowering magic and cunning persuasion. In his comments on Melibea's and Celestina's first meeting in act four, Russell writes:

> Pero el demonio no lo facilita todo sin dar a la maga sus momentos de alarma, hasta el punto de llegar Melibea a denunciarla por lo que es: "¡Quemada seas, alcahueta falsa, *hechizera,* enemiga de la honestidad, causadora de secretos yerros" (IV, 161). Este momento es importantísimo, porque demuestra la extraordinaria resistencia moral de Melibea, no sólo ante las astucias puramente mundanas de la vieja, sino ante los efectos del tremendo maleficio que representa el hilado y la presencia demoníaca dentro de él. Parece mentira que Juan de Valdés censurase a la joven por haberse dejado vencer muy pronto. (263)

According to Russell, Melibea is dominated by the devil through Celestina's magic and is an unwitting and guiltless victim of the *philocaptio.* She is unaware of the cause of the "repentino cambio psicológico" (263) that has come over her, and can only feel the results of the spell that suddenly transforms her from a correct young lady to a passionate woman who is overwhelmed by her desire for Calisto.

James R. Stamm (1988) believes that the young woman's "fácil rendición" destroys the dramatic effectiveness of Calisto's and Melibea's love scene in act fourteen (26), so it appears that contemporary critics are still disturbed by the young woman's *presto vencer* with Calisto. According to Stamm, the young woman's lack of resolve and effective resistance destroys the scene's poetic and romantic qualities: "La escena de amor en el acto XIV de la *Comedia* es brusca, nada poética, casi brutal. La frialdad de Calisto, su burda insistencia y la fácil rendición de Melibea tienden a rebajar los valores líricos y cortesanos – diríamos hoy románticos – en que su pasión ha sido envuelta hasta ahora" (26).

Stamm's criticism of the scene is quite understandable given the way that he describes and interprets Melibea. According to Stamm, Melibea shows herself to be a woman "de carne y hueso" in the book's opening scene, as well as "una mujer inteligente, determinada, sensata y equilibrada" (69). Rojas develops these same characteristics further in act four, so Stamm points out the similarity between the *antiguo auctor*'s Melibea in act one, and Rojas's version of Melibea that appears later in the text: "Mucho más importante, [Rojas] ha sabido desarrollar el personaje de Melibea [en el acto IV] según los pocos indicios que da el Prólogo Dramático [de la primera escena], de manera que no nos cueste creer que es la misma doncella, inteligente y de rápida comprensión, arrebatadiza y básicamente segura de sí y de su posición social" (96).

George Shipley (1975), like Stamm, links Melibea's phantasm in act one with the real Melibea of act four: "Melibea reveals in her first dialogue with Calisto a predilection for the controlled ambiguity of double-directed speech" (325), the same form of expression that she uses with Celestina in act four. An important part of this double-directed speech is Shipley's important observation that Melibea understands and participates in Celestina's deception in act four, where "an unspoken and mutually beneficial accord is reached between the two" women (327). Shipley questions whether Melibea is in reality a naive and inexperienced girl who is overcome by Celestina's cleverness, or an intelligent young woman who understands the old woman's intent and devious methods: "Is [Melibea] innocent and steered into involvement by Celestina, or knowing and concerned about the proper means for achieving a desired end?" (328).

Dorothy Severin (1989) writes that Melibea "resists Calisto's advances vehemently in the first act, but subsequently falls under the spell of Celestina and Calisto" (95). Severin accepts the possiblity of Russell's thesis that Melibea is dominated by Celestina's witchcraft, which would make her a "tragic heroine... caught in a web of events outside her own making and over which she has little control" (101). Nevertheless, Severin also sees an ambivalence in Rojas's view of Melibea, particularly because of her confession in act ten that she has been in love with Calisto from the very first time they met (96).

Miguel Garci-Gómez's interpretation of Calisto's dream in *Celestina*'s opening scene presents a radically different idea about Melibea's role in act one. This reading suggests that there is no need to reconcile Melibea's apparent rejection of Calisto with her later acquiescence because the entire conversation exists only in Calisto's troubled imagination. Melibea's admission in act ten that she was captivated by Calisto should therefore be taken quite seriously, and not as an ambiguous or ambivalent statement. Melibea's *presto vencer* and *fácil rendición* turn out to be illusory because her love for Calisto has existed from the time that he captured her attention when they spoke a few days before the work's opening scene.

What is most striking about Calisto's dream is the simple realization that Melibea does not appear in the *Auto* at all, and that her first participation in the work begins in act four of Rojas's continuation of *Celestina*. The Melibea that we see during the conversation with Celestina therefore has no direct relation to the phantasm that Calisto has imagined in the book's opening scene. Although the plot centers on the young woman and her feelings towards Calisto, she hardly appears until the second half of *Celestina,* and her only direct participation is in acts IV, X, XII, XIV, and XV of the *Comedia,* and acts IV, X, XII, XIV, XV, XVI, XIX, and XX of the *Tragicomedia*.

Melibea's first appearance in the work begins as a silent presence during the conversation between her mother and Celestina in act four. Melibea has been the object of the descriptions and the interest of the other characters throughout the first three acts of *Celestina,* and she now enters the work through the speech of her mother and the procuress. Celestina's first words on the second floor of Pleberio's house are apparently meant for Alisa, but they also acknowledge Melibea's silent but essential role in the scene: "Señora buena, la gracia de Dios sea contigo y con la noble hija" (IV, 153).

Celestina speaks to Alisa about her own advanced age and growing poverty, which would explain why she left her old neighborhood to live in a much poorer area near the river. Nevertheless, her use of proverbs reveals the true motive of her visit. Celestina says that while she is no longer their neighbor, "[L]a distancia de las moradas no despega el *amor* de los coraçones" (IV, 153),[1] so she discreetly refers to the mission assigned to her by Calisto while elic-

---

[1] The *Comedia* refers to "el querer de los coraçones" (IV, 153).

iting pity for her sorrowful economic condition. Alisa willingly leaves her daughter with their former neighbor – "Hija Melibea, quédese esta mujer honrada contigo" (IV, 153) – but Melibea does not speak as long as her mother remains in the house.[2]

It is not until Alisa excuses herself from the room that Celestina shifts the conversation from mother to daughter: "Señora, el perdón sobraría donde el yerro falta; de Dios seas perdonada, que buena compañía me queda. Dios la dexe gozar su noble juventud y florida moçedad, que es [el] tiempo en que más plazeres y mayores deleytes se alcançarán" (IV, 154). Celestina's reference to earthly pleasures and delights again alludes to the reason for her visit, although the young woman remains oblivious to her message.

The conversation between Celestina and Melibea can be divided into four parts, each of which shows a different side of the young woman as she progresses from apparent innocence, to cautious interest, to rage, and finally to covert complicity with the old woman. During the first part of her conversation with Celestina, Melibea exhibits only the very reserved personality of a young girl who respects and defers to her elders, which is quite different from the Melibea that soon surfaces. She demonstrates a youthful lack of judgment when she tells Celestina how old she has gotten, and how she once must have been a beautiful woman. This is such a ridiculous statement that it causes Lucrecia to burst out laughing, which only serves to momentarily upset Melibea.

The first part of their conversation ends when Melibea tries to send Celestina away with discretion and concern for her former

---

[2] Alisa's sudden departure has troubled critics for many years. Alan Deyermond (1977), for example, writes that, "The only possible explanation – in a work justly praised for the convincing motivation of its characters' actions – is that the Devil was in [Celestina's] skein and that at the slightest contact he has taken possession of Alisa's judgment and will" (7). For James R. Stamm (1988), "Dada la mala fama de la vieja, ¿por qué [Alisa] permite que la alcahueta se quede con su hija? ¿Por qué no le da unas monedas por el hilado, y adiós? Es, sin duda, un punto débil en la estructura del acto y de la obra" (90).

The answer is likely far simpler than these scholars believe. Neither Alisa nor Melibea seem to have anything to fear from a visit from their former neighbor. Alisa laughingly calls her "una buena pieça" before she touches the skein (IV, 152), and Melibea notes how old and poor Celestina looks. Even after Celestina returns to the house in act ten, Alisa seems more concerned about robbery or the family's "fama" than about any real harm from the old woman (X, 248). The events in act four respond far more to Christian charity and courtesy to a former neighbor than to Celestina's magic or the supposed structural weaknesses in the work.

neighbor: "Celestina, amiga, yo he holgado mucho en verte y conoscerte; también hasme dado plazer con tus razones. Toma tu dinero y vete con Dios, que me parece que no deves aver comido" (IV, 158). Celestina does not let Melibea off so easily during the second part of their conversation, as she praises Melibea's beauty while gradually revealing that she has not come for her own benefit. Celestina's *habla* confuses the young woman – "Por una parte me alteras y provocas a enojo; por otra me mueves a compasión" (IV, 160) – but Melibea may be more aware of its meaning than she lets on during her transition from apparent innocence to complicity.

Celestina has already mentioned the "noble juventud y florida mocedad [cuando] más plazeres y mayores deleytes se alcançarán" (IV, 154), and also that Melibea should "goz[ar] ... desse cuerpo gracioso" (IV, 158), so the old woman does not hide her intentions. Moreover, as Celestina shifts the discussion away from her advanced age and financial problems, she directly refers to the purpose of her visit: "Assí que donde no ay varón, todo bien fallece. Con mal está el huso quando la barva no anda de suso. Ha venido esto, señora, por lo que dezía de las ajenas necessidades y no mías" (IV, 159). Melibea's response, which should be somewhat restrained during this second and transitional part of their conversation – particularly when Celestina has just mentioned a *varón* – could not be more open ended: "Pide lo que querrás, sea para quien fuere" (IV, 159).

Celestina knows that she can continue her explanation because Melibea's "suave habla y alegre gesto, junto con el aparejo de liberalidad que muestr[a]" (IV, 159) leaves the young woman receptive to the old woman's message. Celestina tells Melibea that she brings news of an "enfermo a muerte" (IV, 159), which under the circumstances could only refer to a young man feeling the effects of an overpowering love. The young woman knows who Celestina is and is well aware of the old woman's profession, so the meaning of her words is unmistakable.

If there are doubts that Melibea understands what Celestina's background is, they are dispelled during her brief fury following Celestina's mention of Calisto's name. This outburst represents the third and most important part of their conversation because at this point Melibea still has the option of rejecting Celestina's message. The young woman calls Celestina an "alcahueta falsa, hechizera" (IV, 161), so the old bawd's behavior should not seem surprising to

Melibea. A short while later Melibea says that, "Bien me avían dicho quién tú eras y avisado de tus propiedades, aunque agora no te conoscía" (IV, 163), but it makes little sense for Melibea to simultaneously affirm ignorance and awareness of her former neighbor's well-known background.

Since Melibea knows Celestina and her profession, and since she probably understood that the old woman was carrying out an assignment from a young man, then what is the reason for Melibea's heated outburst? We must wonder about the statement (or overstatement) of innocence in a young woman who feigns shock when Celestina acts and speaks exactly as a procuress is expected to do, particularly when the old woman has made little effort to hide her intentions. Significantly, Melibea's words during her far too brief outburst reveal the true nature of her anger by suggesting that she is more concerned about the possibility of public dishonor than about the moral implications of a secret love affair with Calisto.

After insulting Celestina, Melibea closes her first statement after hearing Calisto's name by saying, "Por cierto, si no mirasse a mi honestidad, y por no publicar su osadía desse atrevido, yo te hiziera, malvada, que tu razón y vida acabaran en un tiempo" (IV, 162). Melibea does not want to *publicar* Calisto's boldness, which is the same word that she uses to describe her first and only meeting with the young protagonist: "Éste [Calisto] es el quel otro día me vido y començó a desvariar conmigo en razones, haziendo mucho del galán. Dirásle, buena vieja, que si pensó que ya era todo suyo y quedava por él el campo, porque holgué más de consentir sus necedades que castigar su yerro, quise más dexarle por loco que publicar su [grande] atrevimiento" (IV, 162-163).

The first thing we see from Melibea's description of their meeting is that she is not talking about the conversation in the opening scene of act one. Melibea says that she "holg[ó] más de consentir" Calisto's conversation rather than "castigar su yerro," which is the exact opposite of what takes place during her heated outburst in Calisto's dream. What is more, Melibea is unaware of the content of the young man's dream, so a short while later she does not even want Calisto to know that she became upset when Celestina mentioned his name: "Pues, madre, no le des parte de lo que passó a esse cavallero, porque no me tenga por cruel o arrebatada o deshonesta" (IV, 168). Melibea's words and actions would make no sense if Rojas thought that the *Auto* began with a real rather than an imaginary disagreement between the two future lovers.

What has occurred is that Melibea – as she reveals in acts ten and twelve – has also fallen in love with Calisto at first sight during their meeting a few days before. She is concerned about her public honor and is afraid that a lovesick and irrational young man like Calisto might *publicar* the nature of their relationship, so she has to act properly offended at the mention of his name. Melibea therefore insults Celestina and Calisto, but she never follows through with her threats to throw Celestina out of the house. On the contrary, in the midst of her fury the young woman subtly contradicts herself and gives Celestina the opportunity to explain herself and resolve her predicament: "¿Qué dizes, enemiga? Habla que te pueda oýr. ¿Tienes disculpa alguna para satisfazer mi enojo y escusar tu yerro y osadía?" (IV, 163).[3]

Even more revealing is Melibea's next intervention in the conversation, in which she pointedly asks Celestina if there is anything that she can say that would straighten things out between the young woman and Calisto: "¿Qué palabra podías tú querer para esse tal hombre que a mí bien me estuviesse?" (IV, 163). Since Melibea is also in love with Calisto, she is eager to accept Celestina's absurd explanation about Calisto's toothache, which represents the complicity of the fourth and final part of the conversation. Melibea calms down and pretends to believe this ridiculous and transparent ruse, even though she knows that Celestina is incapable of telling the truth: "Por cierto, tantos y *tales* loores me han dicho de tus *falsas* mañas que no sé si crea que pedías oración.... Mi passada altercación me impide a reýr de tu desculpa, que bien sé que ni jura-

---

[3] Shipley correctly emphasizes the contradictions in Melibea's behavior during her conversation with Celestina in act four: "The energetic outburst is a very proper show of indignation; Melibea reacts as a correct maiden should. But we notice that the protestations, though violent, are expressed not as terminal exclamations but rather as interrogations.... Melibea's failure to expel the bawd from her presence (as she had expelled Calisto, for whom Celestina is a 'stand-in') suggests to us that only a code has been broken, not diplomatic relations. The demand for an explanation is more exactly an invitation to open an aternative line of communication in which the real (and indecorous and consequently offensive) base will be replaced by another (fictitious but acceptable) that will make total severance of the interview unnecessary. Thus an unspoken and mutually beneficial accord is reached between the two, a sort of complicity between Celestina and Melibea's undeclared desire, making possible their shared use of the unlikely toothache ruse" (326-27).

mento ni tormento te *hará* dezir verdad, que no es en tu mano" (IV, 165-166).

The talk of helping the sick is nothing more than a linguistic convention that masks the true intent of their conversation and that allows Melibea to say that, "[E]s obra pía y santa sanar los apassionados y enfermos" (IV, 166). Nevertheless, Celestina responds with words that have absolutely nothing to do with healing the sick, and which show that the two women understand each other perfectly: "Y tal enfermo, señora. Por Dios, si bien le conociesses, no le juzgasses por el que as dicho y mostrado con tu yra. En Dios y en mi alma, no tiene hiel; gracias, dos mil; en franqueza, Alexandre; en esfuerço, Hétor; gesto, de un rey; gracioso, alegre, jamás reyna en él tristeza" (IV, 167).

By permitting Celestina's obvious lies, Melibea accepts and participates in Celestina's intrigue. Unlike Pármeno, who could not resist the force of Celestina's speech in act one, Melibea is clever enough to be amused by Celestina's obvious trickery, but she realizes that the only way to communicate with Calisto in secret is through the old bawd. Melibea's and Celestina's conversation is full of double meanings, yet the ambiguous character of their speech allows Melibea to take advantage of Celestina's message with apparent innocence and complete social deniability. Melibea knows that Celestina is not telling the truth and questions her "dubdosa desculpa" (IV, 166), but it is convenient for the young woman to accept and participate in this fiction:

> ¡O quánto me pesa con la falta de mi paciencia!, porque siendo él ignorante y tú innocente, havés padescido las alteraciones de mi ayrada lengua. Pero la mucha razón me relieva de culpa, la qual tu habla sospechosa causó. En pago de tu buen sufrimiento quiero complir tu demanda y darte luego mi cordón. Y porque para screvir la oración no avrá tiempo sin que venga mi madre, si esto no bastare, ven mañana por ella muy secretamente. (IV, 168)

Melibea not only participates in Celestina's fiction, but more importantly she finds a way of extending and expanding on it. She wants Celestina to return "muy secretamente" (IV, 168) the following day because she expects her mother to return to the house soon, so once again she emphasizes the importance of keeping the affair quiet. Celestina assures Melibea that she knows how to keep a secret because she understands Melibea's true concern perfectly: "Mucho me maravillo, señora Melibea, de la dubda que tienes de mi secreto; no temas, que todo lo sé sofrir y encubrir. Que bien veo que tu mucha sospecha echó, como suele, mis razones a la más triste parte" (IV, 168). Melibea's maid Lucrecia also realizes the true meaning of her mistress's words – "(¡Ya, ya, perdida es mi ama! Secretamente quiere que venga Celestina; fraude ay; ¡más le querrá dar que lo dicho!)" (IV, 168) – which Melibea soon confirms to Celestina: "Más haré por tu doliente, si menester fuere, en pago de lo sofrido" (IV, 169).[4]

By the end of the fourth act, Melibea has joined forces with Celestina, but this does not mean that the old woman dominates Melibea's thinking or controls her with her magic. As Stamm has written,

> [E]l diálogo con la alcahueta representa no un sutil engaño, sino una especie de dialéctica en que, con la ayuda de Celestina, la doncella se da cuenta de que está enamorada de Calisto y quiere entregarse al "amor ilícito" que él propuso al principio [de la obra], o por lo menos jugar un poco con el concepto. El procedimiento requiere tiempo y una ayuda para llegar a esta resolución; precisamente la intervención de [Celestina]. (95)

Melibea has unsuccessfully tried to hide the depth of her feelings, but Celestina's words represent the final push needed to convince her to surrender herself to this love. More importantly, Celestina's presence offers the young woman the opportunity to indulge this love without her parents' or her town's knowledge. Me-

---

[4] There are further indications of Melibea's duplicity in Celestina's conversation with Calisto in act six. The old woman knows that Melibea, as an *escondida donzella*, must act as though she had been insulted by the mention of Calisto's name. Nevertheless, her apparent fury demonstrates that she is in love because it reveals that Celestina has struck a raw nerve with the young woman. According to Celestina, "Que a quien más quieren, peor hablan, y si assí no fuesse, ninguna differencia avría entre las públicas, que aman, a las escondidas donzellas, si todas dixiessen sí a la entrada de su primer requerimiento, en viendo que de alguno eran amadas. Las quales, aunque están abrasadas y encendidas de bivos fuegos de amor, por su honestidad muestran un frío esterior, un sossegado vulto, un aplazible desvío, un costante ánimo y casto propósito, unas palabras agras que la propia lengua se maravilla del gran sofrimiento suyo, que la hazen forçosamente confessar el contrario de lo que sienten" (VI, 179).
For an analysis of Melibea's *fingido enojo* in act four, see Heugas (366-67).

libea shows far greater force and drive during this love affair than Calisto does, but she is still a young woman in a traditional, closed society, so Celestina represents a subversive force that allows her to establish a direct and secret relationship with Calisto free of these family and social constraints.

While P. E. Russell (1978) and Alan Deyermond (1977) write about the importance of Celestina's magic in this episode, part of the reason they emphasize this topic is the apparent need to justify Melibea's inexplicable change from act one to act four. Since we know that Melibea does not reject Calisto at the beginning of *Celestina*, it becomes clear that the old woman's spell does not produce a significant change in Melibea after all. The magic spell may play a role in convincing Melibea to accept her physical desire for Calisto, but it is far more likely that the text follows the orthodox Catholic belief that magic cannot control a human being's free will. Celestina's magic therefore works its most important psychological effect on the old woman herself, since she is the only true believer in its power. The supernatural world – whether real or not – plays an essential part in bracing the superstitious old woman during the difficult meeting with Melibea, but it seems to have little or no effect on the young woman.[5]

Melibea's opening dialogue in act ten represents a continuation and expansion of the tendencies that she demonstrates in her only previous appearance in act four of *Celestina*. This scene also suggests that Melibea was captivated when she saw Calisto before the start of the work, and that she did not fall in love with him because of Celestina's magic or diabolic presence. During her monologue at

---

[5] If Melibea had truly been the victim of a *philocaptio*, then there would have been no need for Celestina's persuasive and conspiratorial language throughout act four. Moreover, had Melibea been under Celestina's spell, then she presumably would not have enjoyed the freedom to yell at and insult the old woman. Celestina's position in act four is far too tenuous, and Melibea enjoys far too much verbal autonomy, for the reader to accept the possibility of the overpowering effects of the old woman's *philocaptio*. Pármeno's familiar line in the *Auto* reveals that "todo era burla y mentira" (I, 113), and there is nothing in Rojas's continuation of the work to indicate otherwise.

We may also note that Maxime Chevalier's study of the comments of contemporary readers of *Celestina* indicates that they placed little stock in the old bawd's magical powers: "Sus artes de hechicería no parecen haberles impresionado mucho. Algunos de ellos se refieren a tales habilidades: casi siempre las mencionan de paso, sin concederles gran importancia.... No parecen creer los lectores cultos del siglo XVI en el satanismo y las brujerías de la vieja" (142-43).

the start of act ten, she repeats the word *vista* twice, which reveals that it was Calisto himself and not Celestina who etched the young man's image indelibly into her consciousness:

> ¡O lastimada de mí, o mal proveída donzella! ¿Y no me fuera mejor conceder su petición y demanda ayer a Celestina quando de parte de aquel señor cuya vista me cativó me fue rogado, y contentarle a él, y sanar a mí, que no venir por fuerça a descobrir mi llaga quando no me sea agradescido, quando ya desconfiando de mi buena respuesta aya puesto sus ojos en amor de otra? . . . Pero, ¿cómo lo podré hazer, lastimándome tan cruelmente el ponçoñoso bocado que la vista de su presencia de aquel cavallero me dio? (X, 238)

Melibea realizes that she must be healed of the ailment caused by the sight of Calisto, and that the *galán* might fall in love with another woman if he sets eyes on her. She understands how the process of love works because Calisto and Melibea are both suffering from the same kind of *hereos,* or love sickness, which medieval commentators thought was a visual phenemenon. Doctor Bernardus Gordonius, a thirteenth and fourteenth century professor at Montpellier, wrote that the symptoms of *hereos* "[s]on que pierden el sueño & el comer & el beuer & se enmagresce todo su cuerpo: saluo los ojos" (Seniff 15).[6] According to Couliano (1987), Gordonius wrote that love melancholy does not damage the eyes because

> the very image of the woman has entered the spirit through the eyes and, through the optic nerve, has been transmitted to the sensory spirit that forms comon sense. Transformed into phantasm, the obsessional image has invaded the territory of the three ventricles of the brain, inducing a disordered state of the reasoning faculty (*virtus estimativa*). . . . If the eyes do not partake of the organism's general decay, it is because the spirit uses those

---

[6] Seniff's article includes a fifteenth-century Spanish translation of chapter twenty of the *Lilium Medicinae,* entitled "De amor que se dize hereos." Seniff notes that "There exists one MS and several incunables of the Spanish *Lilio de medicina,* all of which were produced between 1400-1500. It is perhaps significant that the former work, MS 1743, is housed in the Biblioteca Universitaria of Salamanca; might Fernando de Rojas have consulted it during his student days?" (13).

corporeal apertures to try to reestablish contact with the object that was converted into the obsessing phantasm: the woman.[7] (21)

Although some medieval writers thought that heroical love only affected men, Melibea's description of her malady to Celestina reveals that, like Calisto, her illness follows the pattern described by Bernardus Gordonius: "Por cierto, tú lo pides como mujer bien esperta en curar tales enfermedades. Mi mal es de coraçón, la ysquierda teta es su aposentamiento; tiende sus rayos a todas partes. Lo segundo, es nuevamente nascido en mi cuerpo, que no pensé jamás que podía dolor privar el seso como éste haze; túrbame la cara; quítame el comer; no puedo dormir; ningún género de risa querría ver" (X, 241).[8]

There is a precedent for this behavior in the Arcipreste de Talavera, who believes that love melancholy affects both sexes equally: "[N]on ha honbre enamorado que sea dilygente en cosa que sea, salvo en todas las cosas que a su amor pertenescen. . . . E sy un su amigo le ha menester, o fabla con él una hora, nunca palabra entenderá; que non para mientes a lo que fabla por el pensamieto alterado que tyene, pensando en la que ama. Eso mesmo en la muger se falla" (I, XII, 65). Luis Vives, on the other hand, believed that the

---

[7] Andreas Capellanus's *De Amore* also indicates that the eyes are the essential vehicle for producing love melancholy:
> Love is an inborn suffering which results from the sight of, and uncontrolled thinking about, the beauty of the other sex. . . . A careful scrutiny of the truth shows that [love] arises not from any action, but solely from the thought formed by the mind as a result of the thing seen. . . . After that [the lover] starts thinking of her several attractions, contemplating her different parts. . . . He thinks a mere hour an interminable year, because no fulfilment can come quickly enough to a longing heart . . . So this emotion of love is inborn, arising from seeing and thinking. (33, 35)

Capellanus also believes that a blind man cannot fall in love because he cannot establish visual contact with a woman, although he can remain in love if he first saw the woman before he became blind (35).

[8] Burton, like Vives and the Arcipreste, notes that *hereos* is found in women as well as men: "I come at last to that heroical love which is proper to men and women, is a frequent cause of melancholy, and deserves much rather to be called burning lust, than by such an honourable title. . . . [T]his *ferinus insanus amor*, this mad and beastly passion . . . is named by our physicians heroical love, and a more honourable title put upon it, Amor nobilis, as Savanarola styles it, because noble men and women make a common practice of it" (III.2.1.2; 498, 501).

In the Celestinesque genre, Franquila and Claudia in the *Comedia Thebaida* also exhibit the symptoms of love melancholy.

frenesí of love was even stronger in women than in men: "Esta pasión, cuando desenfrenadamente se lleva arrebatados los ánimos de los mortales todos, con desenfreno mayor la lleva los de las mujeres, por cuanto son más impresionables que los de los hombres" (I, XIII, 1051).[9]

Vives may come closest to describing Calisto's and Melibea's relationship because the young woman assumes the place normally reserved for the gentleman in a traditional love affair. While Melibea has always exhibited the "honestidad y vergüença" expected of an "encerrada donzella," her words indicate that her "herido coraçón" and "terrible passión" (X, 238) have completely altered her emotional state: "¡O género femíneo, encogido y frágile! ¿por qué no fue también a las hembras concedido poder descobrir su congoxoso y ardiente amor, como a los varones? Que ni Calisto biviera quexoso ni yo penada" (X, 239). Melibea wants to take the independent and dominant role of the male literary lover, something that she is not able do do until she receives Calisto in her garden in act fourteen, using words that are normally spoken by the courtly lover rather than by his lady: "Es tu sierva, es tu cativa, es la que más tu vida que la suya estima" (XIV, 284).[10]

Since Melibea's illness is of visual origin, she feels better simply by seeing Celestina: "O qué gracioso y agradable me es oýrte; saludable es al enfermo la alegre cara del que le visita" (X, 240). She will also seek to establish visual contact with the man she loves, beginning in act twelve when she regrets that that she is unable to see Calisto in the darkness outside of her window: "¡O mi señor y mi bien todo, quánto más alegre me fuera poder veer tu haz que oýr tu boz!" (XII, 261). In the third and last evening of the *Comedia,* she even tells Calisto how important it is to continue to see him during the day as well as in the evenings: "Señor, ... pues ya soy tu dueña, pues ya no puedes negar mi amor, no me niegues tu vista de día, passando por mi puerta; de noche donde tú ordenares" (XIV, 287).

---

[9] Vives' symptoms of love melancholy are similar to other medieval and Renaissance writers: "Quien estuviere en su sano juicio, al pensar esto, y no esforzarse por no caer jamás en ese frenesí y en esa total ceguera, merecería incurrir en ella para siempre y no hallar ni fin ni medida en sus males, sino que de día y noche fuera acosado por aquella antorcha de Cupido, y que no comiese, ni durmiese, ni viese, ni descansase, y que, a pesar de ser hombre, no desempeñase ninguna función humana" (I, XIII, 1051).

[10] See Lida de Malkiel (370), Swietlicki (3), and Stamm (130).

Although Melibea admits to herself that the cause of her illness is the "vista de su presencia de aquel cavallero" (X, 238), she is less forthright when she begins to speak with Celestina for the second time. She claims to be confused about the nature of her malady, although she suggests that it may be related to her previous conversation with Celestina: "La causa o pensamiento, ... ésta no sabré dezirte, porque ni muerte de deudo ni pérdida de temporales bienes ni sobresalto de visión ni sueño desvariado ni otra cosa puedo sentir que fuesse, salvo [la] alteración que tú me causaste con la demanda que sospeché de parte de aquel cavallero Calisto quando me pediste la oración" (X, 241).

Melibea's words suggest that Celestina's conversation in act four is the cause of the young woman's passion for Calisto, but Celestina realizes that this is not true. The old woman asks Melibea, "¿[T]an mal nombre es el suyo que en sólo ser nombrado trae consigo ponçoña su sonido? No creas que sea éssa la causa de tu sentimiento" (X, 241). Celestina then proceeds to breaks down the last of Melibea's resistance, and the young woman becomes willing to sacrifice her honor for Calisto's love. Much as in act four, Melibea is primarily concerned with maintaining the love affair in secret, although she now accepts the desirability of her relations with Calisto: "[C]ativóme el amor de aquel cavallero [, Lucrecia]; ruégote por Dios se cubra con secreto sello porque yo goze de tan suave amor" (X, 247).

While Melibea wants Celestina to establish contact with Calisto, the young woman does not assume a servile position with the procuress. Melibea calls Celestina "mi nueva maestra, mi fiel secretaria" (X, 245) because they have a variable and interdependent relationship where each one moves from subservience to control and back again. While Melibea is largely dominant in act four, Celestina takes charge in act ten, although Melibea recovers her confidence quickly enough to lie to her mother and again play the role of the young, innocent *encerrada* at the end of the act. Melibea therefore tells her mother at the end of act ten that Celestina will never return to the house because she no longer requires the old woman's assistance.[11] Celestina is an essential vehicle for establishing secret relations with the *galán,* but once Melibea knows that Calisto loves her

---

[11] See Lida de Malkiel (410-13) for Melibea's strength of character and for the relationship between the young woman and her mother Alisa.

and that Celestina will arrange a meeting with him, there is no further need for the old woman.[12]

While we do not witness the first meeting between Calisto and Melibea that takes place outside the text, their conversation in act twelve allows us to reconstruct the result of that first meeting. Melibea begins their discussion in act twelve with proper caution and care as she tells Calisto that he must cease "estos vanos y locos pensamientos" that will surely put her "fama en la balança de las lenguas maldizientes" (XII, 260). Although Celestina has assured her of Calisto's love, Melibea fills the conversation with ambiguous language that will permit her to reaffirm her honor if she concludes that Calisto intends to deceive her. Once again she leaves herself an opening so that she can return to the role of the honest and secretive *encerrada* if anything goes wrong. Calisto must react to a situation controlled entirely by Melibea, but his emotional response fulfills Melibea's expectations and designs perfectly.

As we know, Calisto has been unable to stop thinking about Melibea since their first conversation some days before, and he confirms his malady during the two lovers' conversation outside of Melibea's window: "¡O quantos días antes de agora passados me fue venido esse pensamiento a mi corçón [sic] y por impossible le rechaçava de mi memoria, hasta que ya los rayos illustrantes de tu *muy* claro gesto dieron luz en mis ojos, encendieron mi coraçón, despertaron mi lengua, estendieron mi merecer, acortaron mi covardía, destorcieron mi incogimiento, doblaron mis fuerças" (XII, 261).

Since he is suffering from love sickness, Calisto considers himself unworthy of Melibea and cannot proceed with this love affair unless he knows that she reciprocates his love. Calisto's timid nature indicates anew that Melibea is the principal protagonist of their affair. She runs the greatest risk with her parents and with her society and must make a far greater commitment to their love than he does, but she never hesitates despite the possible consequences of their relationship:

---

[12] Most modern scholars believe that Celestina convinces Melibea to accept Calisto's love, but this interpretation overstates the old woman's role in Rojas's work. Once we understand that Melibea does not reject Calisto in the book's opening scene, then it becomes clear that Celestina's obstacles in acts four and ten are not as formidable as they appeared to be.

> Señor Calisto, tu mucho merecer, tus stremadas gracias, tu alto nascimiento han obrado que, después que de ti ove entera noticia, ningún momento de mi coraçón te partiesses, y aunque muchos días he pugnado por lo dissimular, no he podido tanto que, en tornándome aquella mujer tu dulce nombre a la memoria, no descubriesse mi desseo y viniesse a este lugar y tiempo donde te suplico ordenes y dispongas de mi persona según querrás. (XII, 261-262)[13]

Although Melibea is forceful during her brief love affair with Calisto, she is even more resolute after his horrible death in the darkness outside of her walls. Death has come tragically for Calisto, but it has also come too quickly, and Melibea sees no alternative except to orchestrate her suicide in the same way that she orchestrated the love affair that caused her lover's death. Melibea goes to the top of her father's tower and then asks Lucrecia to tell Pleberio to stand at its foot. With the door locked, she notes that "[t]odo se ha hecho a mi voluntad" (XX, 331), but despite her grief she still has the presence of mind to calmly explain the situation to Pleberio. She understands the terrible tragedy that she is causing her parents, but she is also fully conscious of her culpability in Calisto's death.

Melibea accepted Celestina's initial visit, and once she understood what the old woman wanted, she asked Celestina to return in secret the following day. Melibea also agreed to see Calisto outside of her window during the second evening, and then arranged for him to come to her garden the following night. Ironically, although she has been concerned throughout the work about protecting the secret of her love for Calisto, in the end Melibea sees that she has caused the public clamor that is now felt in the entire city:

> Bien ves y oyes este triste y doloroso sentimiento que toda la cibdad haze. Bien *oyes* este clamor de campanas, este alarido de gentes, este aullido de canes, este [grande] estrépito de armas. De todo esto fue yo [la] causa. Yo cobrí de luto y xergas en este

---

[13] The interpolations in the *Tragicomedia* again suggest that Melibea was in love with Calisto from the very beginning but that she fought this emotion until after her first conversation with Celestina. As her maid Lucrecia tells her, "*Señora, mucho antes de agora tengo sentida tu llaga y callado tu desseo; hame fuertemente dolido tu perdición. Quanto tú más me querías encobrir y celar el fuego que te quemava, tanto más sus llamas se manifestavan en la color de tu cara, en el poco sossiego del coraçón . . .*" (XII, 247).

día quasi la mayor parte de la cibdadana cavallería; yo dexé [hoy] muchos sirvientes descubiertos de señor; yo quité muchas raciones y limosnas a pobres y envergonçantes. (XX, 333)[14]

Melibea's parting words to her father offer us the final confirmation that the young woman fell in love with Calisto prior to her conversation with Celestina in act four. The old woman was able to pry open the secret of Melibea's love, but neither Celestina nor her magic was responsible for creating this emotion:

> Era tanta su pena de amor [de Calisto] y tan poco el lugar para hablarme, que descubrió su passión a una astuta y sagaz mujer que lamavan Celestina. La qual, de su parte venida a mí, sacó mi secreto amor de mi pecho; descobría a ella lo que a mi querida madre encobría; tovo manera cómo ganó mi querer. Ordenó cómo su desseo y el mío oviessen effecto. Si él mucho me amava, no bivió engañado. (XX, 333-34)

With these words, Melibea reaffirms the essential equality of Calisto's and Melibea's passion. Both of them wanted their desires to be fulfilled, and they happily agreed to the fateful assignation that Melibea proposed to Calisto. Her "secreto dolor" cited above is no more than the equivalent of Calisto's "secreto dolor" in the *Auto* (I, 86), as the young woman reiterates the importance that secrecy previously had in their love affair. Unfortunately, Calisto had "tan poco el lugar para habl[ar]" with Melibea, so the young man dies outside of Melibea's walls because he was unable to reproduce the "tan conveniente lugar" of the work's opening scene (I, 86).

As we have noted, Melibea does not appear directly in the *Auto* written by the *antiguo auctor*, so the young woman who appears in *Celestina* is in reality the creation of Fernando de Rojas. In Rojas's continuation of the primitive text, Melibea falls in love with Calisto

---

[14] Severin (1989) believes that this quote shows Melibea to be "almost too eager to accept responsibility for Calisto's death" (103), while Stamm considers it a sign of her self-centeredness (135). According to P. E. Russell, "Melibea, inconsciente víctima del pacto diabólico, se suicida, creyéndose culpable de todo, debido a una irresistible pasión sexual de origen normal y no a los efectos de un maleficio demoníaco.... Fue la *philocaptio*, es decir un hechizo, lo que causó el loco amor de Melibea y, por consiguiente, su muerte" (265).

We have attempted to show in this chapter that although Melibea at first fights the effects of this love, she is perfectly conscious of its cause beginning in act ten, and is serenely aware of her own culpability in Calisto's death.

during their first meeting some time before the start of the work, but she is able to resist this emotion until after her conversation with Celestina in act four. While some critics have been unable to explain how Melibea goes from an absolute rejection of Calisto in the first act to the quick acceptance of his love in acts ten and twelve, this apparent contradiction is resolved by Miguel Garci-Gómez's observation that *Celestina*'s opening scene represents Calisto's lovesick vision of Melibea's phantasm. This interpretation demonstrates that Melibea never changes her attitude towards Calisto, but rather comes to accept her feelings and carry them out to their tragic conclusion.

Given the young woman's strength and determination, it is unsurprising that she kills herself to rejoin her lover after his death. During her brief love affair she has already violated the most important social norms for a young woman in Renaissance Spain, and with her suicide she compounds her transgression by violating fundamental religious laws as well. She is not the victim of Celestina's diabolical influence, but rather of a love sickness that is every bit as powerful as Calisto's and that leads her to consciously participate in Celestina's lies and schemes. Melibea is the true protagonist of the tragic love affair in *Celestina,* and at the end of the work she accepts the seriousness of her transgression and willingly pays the price for her unpardonable behavior.

VI

TOWARDS A NEW VISION OF *CELESTINA*

As we have noted throughout this study of *Celestina,* Miguel Garci-Gómez's interpretation of the *Auto*'s opening scene leads us to a new reading of the work that offers an innovative approach to many of the book's most vexing problems. Calisto's vision of Melibea in scene one resolves a number of apparent contradictions in *Celestina,* particularly some apparent temporal and thematic inconsistencies between the primitive author's *Auto* and Fernando de Rojas's continuation. The result of this new vision of *Celestina* is a more polished and consistent text that facilitates the labor of the modern literary scholar as well as the general reader.

While a new reading of *Celestina*'s opening scene would appear to have a small effect on our understanding of the text as a whole, the orthodox analysis of this scene has created many errors of interpretation that have colored our view of the entire work. The standard explanation for the confusing conversation between Calisto and Melibea in act one has become such an ingrained part of *Celestina* scholarship that critics have not realized how many studies depend on this all-pervasive misinterpretation. Over the years, there have been dozens of influential papers and books that have attempted to explain the textual integrity of the first act, the *Comedy*'s temporal development, Calisto's imputed parodic qualities, Melibea's apparently inexplicable transformation, and the importance of Celestina's magic in the work. Nevertheless, these studies have typically gone astray because they rely on the traditional reading of the first scene, and as a result they have often created more interpretational problems than they have solved.

Despite the uncertainty that the printers' arguments to act one must have caused in the sixteenth century, this study demonstrates that Spanish Celestinesque writers understood that *Celestina*'s opening scene began in Calisto's chamber with the dreams of the already enamored protagonist. The *galán*'s lovesick vision therefore became a common element at the beginning of most Celestinesque texts for well over a century. There are clear rewritings of this scene in the *Comedia Thebaida*, the *Comedia Serafina*, the *Comedia Ypólita*, the *Segunda Celestina*, the *Tercera Celestina*, the *Tragedia Policiana*, the *Comedia Selvagia*, and *La Dorotea*. Significantly, the standard interpretation of the first scene is completely ignored by the Celestinesque tradition.[1]

More importantly for *Celestina* scholars, Fernando de Rojas also understood that the *Auto* begins with Calisto's dream. His continuation of the text in act two, as well as the *Tragicomedia*'s interpolated acts beginning in act fourteen, immediately emphasize Calisto's dreamlike and visionary nature, so there is a return to the *Auto*'s opening scene each time the text is expanded and reworked. While later texts cannot conclusively prove *Celestina*'s structure, it is important to note that Calisto's dream serves as a fundamental intertext as much for Fernando de Rojas as for later Celestinesque writers.

A fundamental part of Calisto's dream is the lack of temporal and spatial separation between the *galán*'s final words to Melibea at the end of scene one, and his subsequent cry for Sempronio at the beginning of scene two. The study of comparable scenes in acts eight and thirteen of Rojas's continuation and in the Celestinesque genre reveals that the master's shout for his servant forms the transition between the opening dream and the continuation of the work. Again, Rojas's work parallels that of later writers in the same genre. The opening conversation thus cannot the work's dramatic prologue, nor is there a subjective temporal separation between *Celestina*'s first two scenes.

With these two scenes united in space and time, it becomes clear that the primitive text is an autonomous and logical narrative

---

[1] The French humanistic comedy of the late sixteenth century followed a similar pattern. According to Madeleine Lazard, "La naissance de l'amour est rapide et brutale. Nous n'y assistons presque jamais. Le jeune homme est d'ordinaire épris dès la premiére scène" (36).

with a precise thematic structure. Some critics have concluded that the *Auto* was significantly altered or damaged when Rojas incorporated it into the complete *Celestina,* but this study suggests that we should accept Rojas's words in "El autor a un su amigo" that, "[A]cordé que todo lo del antiguo auctor fuesse sin división en un aucto o cena incluso" (71). The *Auto* begins in the immaterial and cerebral world of Calisto's vision, and follows Bakhtin's description of the Renaissance grotesque realism, with its rich and dynamic universe centered on the reproductive lower stratum of the human body.

Once we understand Rojas's approach to the *Auto,* we can clarify a number of the apparent inconsistencies between the primitive text and Rojas's complete *Celestina.* Many critics have emphasized the contradictions between the two works, but this study reveals how skillfully Rojas used the primitive text within his own literary creation. The authorial difference between the two works is demonstrated not by these apparent contradictions, but rather by analyzing Rojas's function as the continuator of the text. The *Auto* does not define the exact relationship between Calisto and Melibea, so Rojas uses Pármeno in act two to establish the pre-history of the two future lovers and to provide a logical explanation of Calisto's emotional state in the opening scene.

Critics have long been unable to properly account for the passing of time in *Celestina,* believing that the text demonstrates a subjective time frame, or that it has no understandable time frame at all. We have demonstrated that Rojas's work has a well-defined temporal progression that develops during a seventy-two hour period in the *Comedia,* and for an additional thirty days in the *Tragicomedia.* While the primitive author avoids concrete temporal cues in the *Auto,* Rojas uses the passing of time to organize and separate the work's most important events within discrete twenty-four hour periods. Although the work's temporal development is structured and understandable, the characters continually misinterpret time's inexorable progression. They think they can use time to their advantage, but in reality time works against them and hurries them towards their deaths. The work's temporal development never benefits any of the characters, although they foolishly think otherwise. The years could have helped Pármeno to sever his links with his past, but instead he reaffirms his family's wretched social and moral background when he joins forces with Sempronio. Celestina believes that her age gives her an advantage over her younger *alcahueta* rivals, but in reality it has dulled her senses and increased her desperate need for money, the two problems that lead directly to her violent death.

The study of Calisto confirms Lida de Malkiel's and Dunn's judgment of a complex character who lives in a creative, dreamlike world. He is not a parody of the courtly lover, nor does he mishandle existing texts such as Andreas Capellanus's *De Amore*. The idea of the young protagonist as an absurd caricature underestimates Calisto's innovative use of borrowed speech, and ironically fails to see that Calisto's lovesick behavior is a clear repetition of the Capellanus text that he supposedly mishandles. While some scholars limit the scope of Calisto's development, this study shows that he is a creative, polyglot character who uses previous literary works to create and describe his own love affair. While his literary language confuses Celestina and his servants in the daytime, this is exactly the kind of speech required to communicate with the more cultured and well-read Melibea in the evenings. Calisto is essentially a creature of the darkness who comes to life in the shadowy environment of his gloomy chamber and the nighttime world outside of Melibea's house.

This study also resolves what Juan de Valdés called Melibea's "presto vencer," or the sudden and inexplicable change in her attitude towards Calisto. Modern scholars have not understood why Melibea rejects Calisto one day and then burns with passion for him the next day, although some critics have proposed Celestina's magic or an unrealistic temporal development as possible solutions. Once we know that Melibea's passion begins before the start of the work, and that she never changes her attitude towards Calisto, the young woman takes on a more logical and consistent character. Part *mujer varonil* and part courtly lover, Melibea permits the work's tragic love affair and is largely responsible for its violent conclusion. Unlike the other characters in *Celestina*, Melibea possesses a rare self-awareness that makes her understand her role in the tragedy and her responsibility for the chaos she has created for her family and neighbors.

Celestina is the driving force behind much of the action, and is the work's most fascinating character for modern readers. Nevertheless, this study shows that her role is somewhat diminished in Rojas's continuation of the text, particularly as a result of Melibea's greater self-realization and independence of character. Despite Pármeno's marvelous description of the *puta vieja* in the *Auto* and the indomitable energy she brings to the primitive text, Rojas paints Celestina as a rapidly ageing woman whose best days are far behind her. Her apparent success with Melibea is caused more by the young woman's secret love for Calisto than by the procuress's magic or cunning. Celestina is killed because she remains oblivious to the violent forces that she has set into motion, yet once she is removed from the scene the love affair between Calisto and Melibea continues unaffected.

Because of the importance of Calisto's opening vision for this rereading of *Celestina,* we are left with the vexing problem of why modern scholars were unable to understand this idea before Garci-Gómez's 1985 article. The last of the Spanish Golden Age editions of *Celestina* is dated 1633-1634, and the text was out of print in Spain for 188 years until León Amarita's Madrid edition of 1822.[2] During those years, modern readers lost the cultural and literary cues that suggested a different way to interpret the first scene. Lacking any direct indication in the text, readers relied on the explanation provided by the printers' arguments. Although modern scholars long understood that there were inconsistencies in their reading of the text, these problems were explained away by ideas such as the authorial difference between the anonymous *Auto* and Rojas's continuation.

Although this study demonstrates that Celestinesque writers understood the opening scene correctly, this does not mean that all Renaissance readers saw the episode in the same way. The Burgos printers did not comprehend Calisto's vision, and Juan de Valdés, with his emphasis on Melibea's swift surrender, also seems to have misunderstood the beginning of the work from his exile in Italy. Nevertheless, it is difficult to gauge reader response towards Calisto and Melibea during the Spanish Renaissance because most *comentaristas* wrote about Celestina rather than about the two lovers. Maxime Chevalier, in his study of *Celestina* according to its readers, indicates that there were numerous references to the old woman in contemporary works, but that "[l]as alusiones a Calisto y Melibea son relativamente pocas en los textos del Siglo de Oro" (142). It may simply be that later commentators saw Calisto and Melibea as

---

[2] See Marciales (1985: I, 1-13).

typical literary lovers, so they were drawn towards the unique and more creative Celestina.

This lack of of critical interest during the Spanish Renaissance therefore leaves the Celestinesque genre as the most important textual reaction and commentary on the two young protagonists. Fernando de Rojas and the other Celestinesque writers probably understood Calisto's dream because they lived in an age where love sickness, dreams, and visions formed a normal part of the European world. During love melancholy, the woman's image dominates the lover's mental faculties to such an extent that he thinks of nothing else, and he often exists in a trance-like state where he remains oblivious to the world around him. Although we have noted that the *Paulus* and the *De Amore* represent clear antecedents for Calisto's dream, earlier examples of this convention are legion.

Robert Burton, in *The Anatomy of Melancholy,* provides a long passage that illustrates the continuous presence of lovesick dreams in European literature as far back as the classical period. Burton cites Terence, Virgil, Petronius, Horace, and Achilles Tatius in the classical world, as well as the Renaissance poets Æneas Silvius Piccolomini (Pope Pius II) and George Buchanan (see Appendix I). And while the English author notes that this subject appears repeatedly in amorous literature, there is a much clearer example of the effects of heroical love in the letters of the nun Héloïse (1101-64) to the priest and theologian Abélard (1079-1142), her husband and the father of her child. Much like Calisto, Héloïse is haunted by her absent lover's phantasm, whose sensual image accompanies her even as she sleeps:

> Quant à moi, ces voluptés de l'amour que nous avons goûtées ensemble m'ont été si douces, que le souvenir ne peut m'en déplaire ni même s'effacer de ma mémoire. De quelque côté que je me tourne, elles se présentent, elles s'imposent à mes regards avec les désirs qu'elles réveillent; *leurs trompeuses images n'épargnent même pas mon sommeil* ... Ce n'est pas seulement ce que nouns avons fait, *qui sont si profondément gravés dans mon cœur avec ton image,* que je me retrouve avec toi dans les mêmes lieux, aux mêmes heures, faisant les mêmes choses: *méme en dormant, je ne trouve point de repos.* (Our emphasis, 80-81)

Similar if less scandalous imagery is found in an anonymous Provençal poetess from the twelfth century:

> The whole night long I sigh and dream and waken with a start
> Thinking my friend had roused me from my sleep
> O Heaven! how soon my malady would be cured.
> Should he come to me one night. Ah me!
> Into my curtained chamber he once stole
> Like unto a thief
> Into my chamber richly adorned. . . .
> And hence, unable now to gaze at you admiringly
> I die of pain at my soul's aridity. (Sullerot 57)

Although heroical love was a common topic in medieval writings, the best-known example of this malady occurs in the life and work of Dante. The poet writes in *La vita nuova* that he fell madly in love with Beatrice at the age of nine "quando a li miei occhi apparve prima la gloriosa donna de la mia mente" (1). The mental image of this young woman accompanies him until he sees her again nine years later: "[E] passando per una via, volse li occhi verso quella parte ov'io era molto pauroso, e per la sua ineffabile cortesia ... mi salutòe molto virtuosamente, tanto che me parve allora vedera tutti li termini de la beatitudine" (3). After this chance meeting, the poet begins to suffer the dreams and visions typical of love melancholy, until a dream finally informs him of the death of his beloved.

Tirant lo Blanc shows a comparable process of *abatamiento amoroso* the moment that the knight meets Princess Carmesina in the palace of the Emperor of Constantinople. When Tirant enters the royal chamber, he is listening to the Emperor's words, but his eyes are captivated by the vision of Carmesina:

> Dient l'Emperador tals o semblants paraules les orelles de Tirant estaven atentes a les raons, e los ulls d'altra part contemplaven la gran bellea de Carmesina. E per la gran calor que feia ... estava mig descordada mostrant en los pits dues pomes de paradís que crestallines parien, les quals donaren entrada als ulls de Tirant, que d'Allí avant no trobaren la porta per on eixir, e tostemps foren apresonats en poder de persona lliberta... (CXVII, 374)

After seeing Carmesina, Tirant must immediately lay down in his chamber, his thoughts totally dominated by Carmesina: "Tirant pres llicència de tots e aná-se'n a la posada, entrà-se'n en una cambra e posà lo cap sobre un coixi als peus del llit" (CXVIII, 374).[3]

There are many other texts that allude to the dreamlike symptoms of heroical love. Bernardus Gordonius' (ca. 1258-1318) *Lilio de Medicina* was published in Spanish translations thoughout the fifteenth century, and this medieval treatise contains the chapter devoted to *hereos* that describes the typical Celestinesque protagonist's sickness very precisely. According to the Seville edition of 1495,

> Amor que "hereos" se dize es solicitud melancolica por causa de amor de mugeres. Causas: Desta passion es corrompimiento determinado por la forma & la figura que fuerte mente esta aprehensionada: en alguna muger: & assy concibe la forma & la figura & el modo que cree.... E tanto esta corrompido el iuyzio & la razon que continua mente piensa en ella: & dexa todas sus obras: en tal manera que sy alguno fable con el non lo entiende: por que es en continuo pensamiento....[L]a virtud estimatiua que es la mas alta entre todas las virtudes sensibles manda ala ymaginatiua: & la ymaginatiua manda ala cobdiciable... E por esto se mueue & anda de dia & de noche despreçiando lluuiva & nieve & calor & frio... porque no puede el su cuerpo folgar.... Señales: Son que pierden el sueño & el comer & el beuer & se enamagresce todo su cuerpo" (Seniff 14-15)

As Seniff has written, "A close examination of Barnardus Gordonius' *Lilium Medicinae*... suggests... that Calisto's love melancholy would have been viewed as a fully documented clinical history by a learned audience" (13). Rojas, as a very learned Renaissance reader who was familiar with this medieval notion of heroical love, would have seen that a troubled young lover like Calisto would naturally suffer from trance-like visions of his beloved. While modern readers have noted the apparent lack of contextual and spatial references in scene one, Calisto's agitated mental state and his return to his bed and darkened chamber in scene two confirm that Calisto's conversation with Melibea was caused by the continuous contemplation described by medieval commentators. Moreover, this

---

[3] Rafael Beltrán (1988), writing about Calisto and Tirant, indicates that, "El primer síntoma de la locura de amor es el del abatimiento, y por ello ambos héroes buscan el amparo del lecho para reposar el cuerpo y enjugar sus lágrimas" (41).

behavior was a realistic enough part of Renaissance life that it was not confined to literary characters. Otis H. Green (1963) has noted that early in the sixteenth century Ignatius Loyola experienced the same lovesick trances as Calisto and Héloïse (93). These trances occurred during a period when Loyola was reading novels and books of chivalry, as well as the Life of Christ and the Lives of the Saints. Despite his interest in hagiography, Loyola's autobiography reveals that he suffered from worldly visions and physical desires:

> Of the many vain things that presented themselves to him, one took such possession of his heart that without realizing it he could spend two, three, or even four hours on end thinking of it, fancying what he would have to do in the service of a certain lady, of the means he would take to reach the country where she was living, of the verses, the promises he would make her, the deeds of gallantry he would do in her service. (9)

Literature inspired Loyola's wordly thoughts and visions, while his religious readings produced spiritual "thoughts [that] also lasted a good while" (10). Loyola eventually understands "the difference between the two spirits that moved him, the one being from the evil spirit, the other from God" (10), and he decides to abandon his interest in the flesh in favor of visions of God and the Virgin. Loyola's fantasy of a beautiful woman is the precise opposite of his religious visions, but they were equally believable in the Spanish Renaissance. A contemporary reader would accept Calisto's fictional dreams the same way he would understand Loyola's earthly and divine apparitions. Calisto's tendency to "holga[r] con lo escuro" appears to be a worldly degeneration of the *noche escura* that San Juan de la Cruz says is necessary to reach union with God, and both concepts coexist within the same social and philosophical environment.[4]

As revealed in the writings of Héloïse, Dante, and Loyola, there is no separation between lovesick behavior in life and literature. In

---

[4] San Juan writes that, "el alma ... salió sacándola Dios sólo por amor dél, inflamada en su amor *en su noche escura* que es la privación y purgación de todos sus apetitos sensuales acerca de todas las cosas exteriores del mundo y de las que eran deleitables a su carne, y también de los gustos de su voluntad, lo cual todo se hace en esta purgación del sentido" (1984: 64). The nature of Calisto's dreams is just the opposite of religious visions because his dreams represent an absolute surrender to the sensual and earthly pleasures that San Juan says must be abandoned.

fact, the most precise description of Calisto's love melancholy is found in Francisco López de Villalobos's gloss to his own translation of the *Anfitrión* (1544), a text that represents a literal combination of literary and scientific commentary.[5] Villalobos – the personal physician to Fernando el Católico and the Emperor Carlos V – writes that the woman's phantasy dominates not only the young lover's daytime thoughts, but also his his dreams up to moment of awakening:

> Entre las potencias y sentidos interiores hay una que se llama imaginativa ... [que] es maestra de hacer imágenes y componerlas. ... Esta imaginativa adolesce algunas veces de un género de locura que se llama alienación, y es por parte de algún malo y rebelde humor que ofusca y enturbia el espíritu do se hacen las imágenes, fórmase allí la imagen falsa ... [y] si la tiene, es mentirosa y enajenada la imaginación, y cuanto piensan, todo es del metal de aquella imagen que allí está, de aquello habla el alienado, y en ello está rebatado y trasportado de tal manera, que no oye ni ve ni entiende cosa que le digan. ... Los enamorados son desta materia: que la imagen de su amiga tienen siempre figurada y fija dentro de sus pensamientos, por donde no pueden ocupar jamás la imaginación en otra cosa; en esta imagen ... están trasportados y rebatados todas las horas; con ella hablan, della cantan y della lloran, con ella comen y duermen y despiertan. (488-89)

Although this study presents a new and perhaps controversial reading of *Celestina*, it also attempts to buttress its arguments with solid textual evidence and extensive internal and external corroborating documentation. Calisto's initial dream, which forms the keystone of this entire study, is shown to follow the tradition of love melancholy in European letters previously found in classical literature, Héloïse's letters to Abélard, Andreas Capellanus, Provençal poetry, Bernardus Gordonius, the *Paulus*, Dante's *La vita nuova*,

---

[5] Coincidentally, Villalobos started to write at the University of Salamanca at about the same time that Rojas would have been completing *Celestina*. According to Adolfo de Castro, "La primera de [sus obras] fue una que se intitula *Sumario de la medicina, en romance trovado, con un tratado sobre las pestíferas bulas, por el licenciado* Villalobos, *estudiante de Salamanca, hecho a contemplación del muy magnífico e ilustre señor el marqués de Astorga*. (Salamanca, a expensas de Antonio de Barreda, librero, año de 1498)" (xxii).

and *Tirant lo Blanc*. We have also demonstrated that Calisto twice wakes up from lovesick dreams about Melibea in Rojas's continuation of *Celestina*, and that the *galán* immediately calls out to his servants as he did at the beginning of the first act. Moreover, Calisto reveals during the work's first morning that "En sueños la ve tantas noches" (VI, 186), clearly indicating that he has been dreaming about Melibea during the previous evenings.

Hereos, as a realistic expression of a young man's love, served to eliminate the boundaries between literature and life for contemporary readers of *Celestina*. Ironically, since our ideas and understanding have changed over the centuries, love melancholy has created a barrier of comprehension for the modern reader. The unusual character and difficult conversation of Calisto's dream, along with the printers' misleading arguments, have served to confuse generations of *Celestina* scholars. Literary critics have long addressed the problems and contradictions that plague the traditional interpretation of the first scene, but there has been insufficient effort to question the very basis of this reading. Too many scholars have been content to make *Celestina* fit their particular views and theories, rather than creatively adapt these views and theories to fit the text's literary reality. Garci-Gómez's reading of scene one provides a vision of a richer and less problematical *Celestina*, along with a critical framework that will continue to develop as we approach the quincentennial of Fernando de Rojas's *Comedia de Calisto y Melibea*.

APPENDIX I

Robert Burton. *The Anatomy of Melancholy.* (Third Partition, Section 2, Member 3: "Symptoms of Love-Melancholy, in Body, in Mind, good, bad, &c.")

Howsoever his present state be pleasing or displeasing, 'tis continuate so long as he loves, he can do nothing, think of nothing but her; desire hath no rest, she is his cynosure, hesperus and vesper, his morning and evening star, his goddess, his mistress, his life, his soul, his everything; dreaming, waking, she is always in his mouth. . . . When Thais took leave of Phædria, – *mi Phæddria, et nunquid aliud vis?* Sweetheart (she said) will you command me any further service: He readily replied, and gave his charge,

–"egone quid velim?
Dies noctesque ames me, me desideres,
Me somnies, me expectes, me cogites,
Me speres, me te oblected, mecum tota sis,
Meus fac postremò animus, quando ego sum tuus."

"Dost ask (my dear) what service I will have?
To love me day and night is all I crave.
To dream on me, to expect, to think on me,
Depend and hope, still covet me to see,
Delight thyself in me, be wholly mine,
For know, my love, that I am wholy thine." [Terence]

But all this needed not, you will say; if she affect once, she will be his, settle her love on him, on him alone,

−"illum absens absentem
auditque videtque"−

["Seeing and hearing him,
though they be parted" (Virgil)]

she can, she must think and dream of nought else but him, continually of him, as did Orpheus on his Eurydice,

"Te dulcis conjux, te solo in litore mecum,
Te veniente die, te discendente canebam."

"On thee sweet wife was all my song,
Morn, evening, and all along." [Virgil]

... Clitophon, in the first book of Achilles Tatius, complaineth how that his mistress Leucippe, tormented him much more in the night than in the day. "For all day long he had some object or other to distract his senses, but in the night all ran upon her. All night long he lay awake, and could think of nothing else but her, he could not get her out of his mind; towards morning, sleep took a little pity on him, he slumbered awhile, but all his dreams were of her."

−"te nocte sub atrâ
Alloquor, amplector, falsaque in imagine somni,
Gaudia solicitam palpant evanida mentem."

"In the dark night I speak, embrace, and find
That fading joys deceive my careful mind." [Buchanan]

The same complaint Eurialus makes to his Lucretia, "day and night I think of thee, I wish for thee, I talk of thee, call on thee, look for thee, hope for thee, delight myself in thee, day and night I love thee" [Æneas Silvius Piccolomini].

"Nec mihi vespere
Surgente decedunt amores,
Nec rapidum figiente solem."

Morning, evening, all is alike with me, I have restless thoughts, "*Te vigilans oculis, animo te nocte requiro*" ["Thee with waking eyes and anxious mind I follow all night" (Petronius)] ... I live and breathe in thee, I wish for thee.

> "O niveam quæ te poterit mihi redere lucem,
> O mihi felicem terque quaterque diem."

"O happy day that shall restore thee to my sight" [Horace]. In the meantime he raves on her; her sweet face, eyes, actions, gestures, hands, feet, speech, length, breadth, height, depth, and the rest of her dimensions, are so surveyed, measured, and taken, by that Astrolabe of phantasy, and that so violently sometimes, with such earnestness and eagerness, such continuance, so strong an imagination, that at length he thinks he sees her indeed; he talks with her, he embraceth her, Ixion-like. . . I see and meditate of nought but Leucippe. Be she present or absent, all is one. (558-59)

Interpolated English translations from *The Anatomy of Melancholy*. Ed. Floyd Dell and Paul Jordan-Smith. New York: Tudor Publishing Company (1951): 732-33.

BIBLIOGRAPHY

Abélard and Héloïse. *Lettres complètes d'Abélard et d'Héloïse.* Trans. M. Gréard. Paris: Garnier Frères, no year given.
Anonymous. *La comedia llamada Serafina.* Ed. Glen F. Dille. Carbondale and Edwardsville: Southern Illinois University Press, 1979.
Anonymous. *La comedia Thebaida.* Ed. G. D. Trotter and Keith Whinnom. London: Tamesis Books, 1969.
Anonymous. *La comedia Ypólita.* Ed. Philip Earle Douglass. Philadelphia: U Pennsylvania P, 1929.
Asensio, Manuel. "El tiempo en *La Celestina.*" *Hispanic Review* XX (1952): 28-43.
———. "A Rejoinder [to Stephen Gilman]." *Hispanic Review* XXI (1953): 45-50.
Barbera, R. E. "Medieval Iconography in *La Celestina.*" *Romanic Review* LXI (1970): 5-13.
Bakhtin, Mikhail. *Rabelais and His World.* Trans. Helene Iswolsky. Bloomingdale: Indiana UP, 1984.
———. *The Dialogic Imagination.* Austin: U Texas P, 1990.
Bataillon, Marcel. La Célestine *selon Fernando de Rojas.* Paris: Didier, 1961.
———. *Défense et illustration du sens littéral.* London: Modern Humanities Research Association, 1967.
Beltrán, Rafael. "Paralelismos en los enamoramientos de Calisto y Tirant lo Blanc: los primeros síntomas del 'mal de amar.'" *Celestinesca* XII (1988): 33-53.
Boccaccio, Giovanni. *Teseida delle nozze d'Emilia.* Ed. Vittore Branca. *Tutte le opere di Giovanni Boccaccio.* Verona: Mondadori (1964): 231-664.
———. *The Life of Dante.* Trans. James Robinson Smith. *The Lives of Dante.* New York: Russell & Russell (1968): 9-78.
Burton, Robert. *The Anatomy of Melancholy.* London: Chatto and Windus, 1907.
Capellanus, Andreas. *Andreas Capellanus on Love.* Trans. P. G. Walsh. London: Duckworth, 1982.
Castells, Ricardo. "El mal de amores de Calisto y el diagnóstico de Eras y Crato, médicos." *Hispania* 76 (1993): 18-23.
Castiglione, Baldassarre. *Il libro del Cortegiano.* Ed. Ettore Bonora. Milano: Grande Universale Mursia, 1972.
Cervantes, Miguel de. *Don Quijote de la Mancha.* Ed. Martín de Riquer. Barcelona: Editoria Juventud, 1971. 2 vols.
Chaucer, Geoffrey. *The Canterbury Tales.* Ed. V. A. Kolve and Glending Olson. New York: W. W. Norton, 1989.
Chevalier, Maxime. *Lectura y lectores en la España de los siglos XVI y XVII.* Madrid: Turner, 1976.

Corcoran, C. J. "Glorified Body." *New Catholic Encyclopedia*. New York: McGraw Hill, 1967. Vol. VI, 512-13.
Couliano, Ioan P. *Eros and Magic in the Renaissance*. Trans. Margaret Cook. Chicago and London: U of Chicago P, 1987.
Dante Alighieri. *La vita nuova*. Ed. Kenneth McKenzie. New York: D.C. Heath, 1922.
de Castro, Adolfo. "Apuntes biográficos." Madrid: BAE 36 (1950): xi-xxiv.
Deyermond, A. D. "The Text-Book Mishandled: Andreas Capellanus and the Opening Scene of *La Celestina*." *Neophilologus* XLI (1961): 218-221.
―――. "*Hilado-Cordón-Cadena*: Symbolic Equivalence in *La Celestina*." *Celestinesca* I (May, 1977): 6-12.
Dunn, Peter N. *Fernando de Rojas*. Boston: Twayne, 1975.
Faulhaber, Charles B. "The Hawk in Melibea's Garden." *Hispanic Review* XLV (1977): 435-50.
Fernández, Sebastián. *Tragedia Policiana*. Madrid: Nueva Biblioteca de Autores Españoles, 1910, vol. XIV.
Fox, Ruth A. *The Tangled Chain: The Structure of Disorder in* The Anatomy of Melancholy. Berkeley: U California P, 1976.
Fraker, Charles F. Celestina: *Genre and Rhetoric*. London: Tamesis, 1990.
Garci-Gómez, Miguel. "El sueño de Calisto." *Celestinesca* IX (1985): 11-22.
―――. "Ascendencia y trascendencia del neblí de Calisto." *Revista de Literatura* XLIX, 97 (1987): 5-21.
Gilman, Stephen. "El tiempo y el género literario en *La Celestina*." *Revista de Filología Hispánica* VII (1945): 147-59.
―――. "A Propos of 'El tiempo en *La Celestina*' by Manuel Asensio." *Hispanic Review* XXI (1953): 42-45.
―――. *The Art of* La Celestina. Madison: U of Wisconsin P, 1956.
―――. *The Spain of Fernando de Rojas*. Princeton UP, 1972.
Goldberg, Harriet. "The Dream Report as a Literary Device in Medieval Hispanic Literature." *Hispania* LXVI (1983): 21-31.
Gómez de Toledo, Gaspar. *Tercera parte de la tragicomedia de Celestina*. Ed. Mac E. Barrick. Philadelphia: U of Pennsylvania P, 1973.
Green, Otis H. *Spain and the Western Tradition*. Madison: U Wisconsin P, 1963. Volume I.
―――. "The Artistic Originality of *La Celestina*." *Hispanic Review* XXXIII (1965): 15-31.
Hebreo, León. *Diálogos de amor*. Trans. Inca Garcilaso de la Vega. Madrid: BAE 132 (1965): 3-227.
Heugas, Pierre. La Célestine *et sa descendance directe*. Bordeaux: Institut d'Études Ibériques et Ibéro-Américaines, 1973.
Ignatius Loyola, Saint. *St. Ignatius' Own Story as told to Luis González de Cámara*. Trans. William J. Young, S. J. Chicago: Loyola UP, 1956.
Juan de la Cruz, San. *Poesías completas*. Mexico: Editorial Origen, 1984.
Lacarra, María Eugenia. "La parodia de la ficción sentimental en la *Celestina*." *Celestinesca* XIII (1989): 11-29.
Lazard, Medeleine. *La comèdie humaniste au XVIe siècle et ses personnages*. Vêndome: Presses Universitaires de France, 1978.
Legge, M. Dominica. "Toothache and Courtly Love." *French Studies* IV (1950): 50-54.
Lewis, C. S. *The Allegory of Love: A Study in Medieval Tradition*. Oxford: Clarendon Press, 1936.
Lida de Malkiel, María Rosa. *La originalidad artística de* La Celestina. Buenos Aires: EUDEBA, 1962; rpt. 1970.

Lowes, John Livingston. "The Loveres Maladye of Hereos." *Modern Philology* XI (1914): 491-546.
Marciales, Miguel. *Sobre problemas rojanos y celestinescos*. Mérida, Venezuela: Universidad de los Andes, 1983.
———. *Celestina: Tragicomedia de Calisto y Melibea*. Introducción al ciudado de Brian Dutton y Joseph T. Snow. 2 vols. Urbana and Chicago: Illinois Medieval Monographs, 1985.
Martin, June Hall. *Love's Fools: Aucassin, Troilus, Calisto and the Parody of the Courtly Lover*. London: Tamesis, 1972.
Martínez de Toledo, Alfonso. *Arcipreste de Talavera o Corbacho*. Ed. J. González Muela. Madrid: Castalia, 1970.
Martorell, Joanot and Martí Joan de Galba. *Tirant lo Blanc*. Ed. Martí de Riquer. Barcelona: Editorial Ariel, 1979.
Menéndez Pelayo, Marcelino. *Orígenes de la novela*. Madrid: Nueva Biblioteca de Autores Españoles, 1910. Rpt. *La Celestina*. Madrid: Austral, 1979.
Redle, M. J. "Beatific Vision." *New Catholic Encyclopedia*. New York: McGraw Hill, 1967. Vol. II, 186-93.
Riquer, Martín de. "Fernando de Rojas y *La Celestina*." *Revista de Filología Española* XLI (1957): 373-95.
Rojas, Fernando de. *La Celestina*. Ed. Dorothy S. Severin. Notes in collaboration with Maite Cabello. Madrid: Cátedra, 1990.
Rueda, Lope de. *Comedia llamada Eufemia*. In *Teatro completo*. Ed. Angeles Cardona de Gibert. Barcelona: Bruguera, 1979.
Rumea, A. "Introduction à Célestine: 'una cosa bien escusada...'." *Les Langues Neo-latines* LX, 176 (1966): 1-26.
Russell, P. E. *Temas de* La Celestina *y otros estudios del* Cid *al* Quijote. Barcelona: Ariel, 1978.
Sánchez Sánchez-Serrano, Antonio and María Remedios Prieto de la Iglesia. "Fernando de Rojas acabó la *Comedia de Calisto y Melibea*." *Revista de Literatura* LI, 101 (1989): 21-54.
Seniff, Dennis P. "Bernardo Gordonio's *Lilio de Medicina:* A Possible Source of *Celestina?*" *Celestinesca* X (1986): 13-18.
Severin, Dorothy Sherman. *Memory in* La Celestina. London: Tamesis Books, 1970.
———. *Tragicomedy and Novelistic Discourse in* Celestina. Cambridge: Cambridge UP, 1989.
Shipley, George. "Concerting through Conceit." *Modern Language Review* LXX (1975): 324-32.
Silva, Feliciano de. *Segunda Celestina*. Ed. Consolación Baranda. Madrid: Cátedra, 1988.
Solomon, Michael. "Calisto's Ailment: Bitextual Diagnostics and Parody in *Celestina*." *Revista de Estudios Hispánicos* XXIII (1989): 41-64.
Soufas, Teresa Scott. *Melancholy and the Secular Mind in Spanish Golden Age Literature*. Columbia: U Missouri P, 1990.
Stamm, James R. *La estructura de* La Celestina. Salamanca: Ediciones de la Universidad de Salamanca, 1988.
Sullerot, Evelyne. *Women in Love: Eight Centuries of Femenine Writing*. Trans. Helen R. Lane. Garden City, NY: Doubleday and Company, 1979.
Swietlicki, Catherine. "Rojas's View of Women: A Reanalysis of *La Celestina*." *Hispanófila* LXXXI (1985): 1-13.
Truesdell, W. D. "The Hortus Conclusus Tradition, and the Implications of its Absence in the *Celestina*." *Kentucky Romance Quarterly* XX (1973): 257-77.
Valdés, Juan de. *Diálogo de la lengua*. Ed. Juan M. Lope Blanch. Madrid: Castalia, 1969.

Vega, Garcilaso de la. *Poesías castellanas completas.* Ed. Elias L. Rivers. Madrid: Castalia, 1987.
Vega, Lope de. *La Dorotea.* Ed. Edwin S. Morby. Madrid: Castalia, 1987.
Veres D'Ocón, Ernesto. "Los retratos de Dulcinea y Maritornes." *Anales Cervantinos* I (1951): 251-71.
Vian Herrero, Ana. "El pensamiento mágico en *Celestina,* 'instrumento de lid o contienda'." *Celestinesca* XIV (1990): 41-91.
Villalobos, Francisco López de. *Anfitrión, comedia de Plauto.* Madrid: BAE 36 (1950): 461-93.
Villegas Selvago, Alonso de. *La comedia llamada Selvagia.* Madrid: Colección de libros raros o curiosos, 1873, vol. V.
Vives, Luis. *Formación de la mujer cristiana.* Madrid: Aguilar (1947): I, 985-1175.
Weinberg, F. M. "Aspects of Symbolism in *La Celestina.*" *MLN* LXXXVI (1971): 136-53.
West, Geoffrey. "The Unseemliness of Calisto's Toothache." *Celestinesca* III (May, 1979): 3-10.

NORTH CAROLINA STUDIES IN THE ROMANCE LANGUAGES AND LITERATURES

I.S.B.N. Prefix 0-8078-

Recent Titles

TWO AGAINST TIME. *A Study of the Very Present Worlds of Paul Claudel and Charles Péguy*, by Joy Nachod Humes. 1978. (No. 200). -9200-9.
TECHNIQUES OF IRONY IN ANATOLE FRANCE. Essay on *Les Sept Femmes de la Barbe-Bleue*, by Diane Wolfe Levy. 1978. (No. 201). -9201-7.
THE PERIPHRASTIC FUTURES FORMED BY THE ROMANCE REFLEXES OF "VADO (AD)" PLUS INFINITIVE, by James Joseph Champion. 1978. (No. 202). -9202-S.
THE EVOLUTION OF THE LATIN /b/-/u/ MERGER: A Quantitative and Comparative Analysis of the B-V Alternation in Latin inscriptions, by Joseph Louis Barbarino. 1978. (No. 203). -9203-3.
METAPHORIC NARRATION: THE STRUCTURE AND FUNCTION OF METAPHORS IN "A LA RECHERCHE DU TEMPS PERDU", by Inge Karalus Crosman. 1978. (No. 204). -9204-1.
LE VAIN SIECLE GUERPIR. A Literary Approach to Sainthood through Old French Hagiography of the Twelfth Century, by Phyllis Johnson and Brigitte Cazelles. 1979. (No. 205). -9205-X.
THE POETRY OF CHANGE: A STUDY OF THE SURREALIST WORKS OF BENJAMIN PÉRET, by Julia Field Costich. 1979. (No. 206). -9206-8.
NARRATIVE PERSPECTIVE IN THE POST-CIVIL WAR NOVELS OF FRANCISCO AYALA "MUERTES DE PERRO" AND "EL FONDO DEL VASO", by Maryellen Bieder. 1979. (No. 207). -9207-6.
RABELAIS: HOMO LOGOS, by Alice Fiola Berry. 1979. (No. 208). -9208-4.
"DUEÑAS" AND DONCELLAS": A STUDY OF THE DOÑA RODRÍGUEZ EPISODE IN "DON QUIJOTE", by Conchita Herdman Marianella. 1979. (No. 209). -9209-2.
PIERRE BOAISTUAU'S "HISTOIRES TRAGIQUES": A STUDY OF NARRATIVE FORM AND TRAGIC VISION, by Richard A. Carr. 1979. (No. 210). -9210-6.
REALITY AND EXPRESSION IN THE POETRY OF CARLOS PELLICER, by George Melnykovich. 1979. (No. 211). -9211-4.
MEDIEVAL MAN, HIS UNDERSTANDING OF HIMSELF, HIS SOCIETY, AND THE WORLD, by Urban T. Holmes, Jr. 1980. (No. 212). -9212-2.
MÉMOIRES SUR LA LIBRAIRIE ET SUR LA LIBERTÉ DE LA PRESSE, introduction and notes by Graham E. Rodmell. 1979. (No. 213). -9213-0.
THE FICTIONS OF THE SELF. THE EARLY WORKS OF MAURICE BARRES, by Gordon Shenton. 1979. (No. 214). -9214-9.
CECCO ANGIOLIERI. A STUDY, by Gifford P. Orwen. 1979. (No. 215). -9215-7.
THE INSTRUCTIONS OF SAINT LOUIS: A CRITICAL TEXT, by David O'Connell. 1979. (No. 216). -9216-5.
ARTFUL ELOQUENCE, JEAN LEMAIRE DE BELGES AND THE RHETORICAL TRADITION, by Michael F. O. Jenkins. 1980. (No. 217). -9217-3.
A CONCORDANCE TO MARIVAUX'S COMEDIES IN PROSE, edited by Donald C. Spinelli. 1979. (No. 218). 4 volumes, -9218-1 (set), -9219-X (v. 1), -9220-3 (v. 2); -9221-1 (v. 3); -9222-X (v. 4).
ABYSMAL GAMES IN THE NOVELS OF SAMUEL BECKETT, by Angela B. Moorjani. 1982. (No. 219). -9223-8.
GERMAIN NOUVEAU DIT HUMILIS: ÉTUDE BIOGRAPHIQUE, par Alexandre L. Amprimoz. 1983. (No. 220). -9224-6.
THE "VIE DE SAINT ALEXIS" IN THE TWELFTH AND THIRTEENTH CENTURIES: AN EDITION AND COMMENTARY, by Alison Goddard Elliot. 1983. (No. 221). -9225-4.
THE BROKEN ANGEL: MYTH AND METHOD IN VALÉRY, by Ursula Franklin. 1984. (No. 222). -9226-2.

When ordering please cite the *ISBN Prefix* plus the last four digits for each title.

Send orders to: University of North Carolina Press
P.O. Box 2288
CB# 6215
Chapel Hill, NC 27515-2288
U.S.A.

NORTH CAROLINA STUDIES IN THE ROMANCE LANGUAGES AND LITERATURES

I.S.B.N. Prefix 0-8078-

Recent Titles

READING VOLTAIRE'S CONTES: A SEMIOTICS OF PHILOSOPHICAL NARRATION, by Carol Sherman. 1985. (No. 223). -9227-0.

THE STATUS OF THE READING SUBJECT IN THE "LIBRO DE BUEN AMOR", by Marina Scordilis Brownlee. 1985. (No. 224). -9228-9.

MARTORELL'S TIRANT LO BLANCH: A PROGRAM FOR MILITARY AND SOCIAL REFORM IN FIFTEENTH-CENTURY CHRISTENDOM, by Edward T. Aylward. 1985. (No. 225). -9229-7.

NOVEL LIVES: THE FICTIONAL AUTOBIOGRAPHIES OF GUILLERMO CABRERA INFANTE AND MARIO VARGAS LLOSA, by Rosemary Geisdorfer Feal. 1986. (No. 226). -9230-0.

SOCIAL REALISM IN THE ARGENTINE NARRATIVE, by David William Foster. 1986. (No. 227). -9231-9.

HALF-TOLD TALES: DILEMMAS OF MEANING IN THREE FRENCH NOVELS, by Philip Stewart. 1987. (No. 228). -9232-7.

POLITIQUES DE L'ECRITURE BATAILLE/DERRIDA: le sens du sacré dans la pensée française du surréalisme à nos jours, par Jean-Michel Heimonet. 1987. (No. 229). -9233-5.

GOD, THE QUEST, THE HERO: THEMATIC STRUCTURES IN BECKETT'S FICTION, by Laura Barge. 1988. (No. 230). -9235-1.

THE NAME GAME. WRITING/FADING WRITER IN "DE DONDE SON LOS CANTANTES", by Oscar Montero. 1988. (No. 231). -9236-X.

GIL VICENTE AND THE DEVELOPMENT OF THE COMEDIA, by René Pedro Garay. 1988. (No. 232). -9234-3.

HACIA UNA POÉTICA DEL RELATO DIDÁCTICO: OCHO ESTUDIOS SOBRE "EL CONDE LUCANOR", por Aníbal A. Biglieri. 1989. (No. 233). -9237-8.

A POETICS OF ART CRITICISM: THE CASE OF BAUDELAIRE, by Timothy Raser. 1989. (No. 234). -9238-6.

UMA CONCORDÃNCIA DO ROMANCE "GRANDE SERTÃO: VEREDAS" DE JOÃO GUIMARÃES ROSA, by Myriam Ramsey and Paul Dixon. 1989. (No. 235). Microfiche, -9239-4.

CYCLOPEAN SONG: MELANCHOLY AND AESTHETICISM IN GÓNGORA S "FÁBULA DE POLIFEMO Y GALATEA", by Kathleen Hunt Dolan. 1990. (No. 236). -9240-8.

THE "SYNTHESIS" NOVEL IN LATIN AMERICA. A STUDY ON JOÃO GUIMARÃES ROSA'S "GRANDE SERTÃO: VEREDAS", by Eduardo de Faria Coutinho. 1991. (No. 237). -9241-6.

IMPERMANENT STRUCTURES. SEMIOTIC READINGS OF NELSON RODRIGUES' "VESTIDO DE NOIVA", "ÁLBUM DE FAMÍLIA", AND "ANJO NEGRO", by Fred M. Clark. 1991. (No. 238). -9242-4.

"EL ÁNGEL DEL HOGAR". GALDÓS AND THE IDEOLOGY OF DOMESTICITY IN SPAIN, by Bridget A. Aldaraca. 1991. (No. 239). -9243-2.

IN THE PRESENCE OF MYSTERY: MODERNIST FICTION AND THE OCCULT, by Howard M. Fraser. 1992. (No. 240). -9244-0.

THE NOBLE MERCHANT: PROBLEMS OF GENRE AND LINEAGE IN "HERVIS DE MES", by Catherine M. Jones. 1993. (No. 241). -9245-9.

JORGE LUIS BORGES AND HIS PREDECESSORS OR NOTES TOWARDS A MATERIALIST HISTORY OF LINGUISTIC IDEALISM, by Malcolm K. Read. 1993. (No. 242). -9246-7.

DISCOVERING THE COMIC IN "DON QUIXOTE", by Laura J. Gorfkle. 1993. (No. 243). -9247-5.

THE ARCHITECTURE OF IMAGERY IN ALBERTO MORAVIA'S FICTION, by Janice M. Kozma. 1993. (No. 244). -9248-3.

THE "LIBRO DE ALEXANDRE". MEDIEVAL EPIC AND SILVER LATIN, by Charles F. Fraker. 1993. (No. 245). -9249-1.

THE ROMANTIC IMAGINATION IN THE WORKS OF GUSTAVO ADOLFO BÉCQUER, by B. Brant Bynum. 1993. (No. 246). -9250-5.

MYSTIFICATION ET CRÉATIVITÉ DANS L'OEUVRE ROMANESQUE DE MARGUERITE YOURCENAR, par Beatrice Ness. 1994. (No. 247). -9251-3.

When ordering please cite the *ISBN Prefix* plus the last four digits for each title.

Send orders to: University of North Carolina Press
P.O. Box 2288
CB# 6215
Chapel Hill, NC 27515-2288
U.S.A.

The Department of Romance Studies Digital Arts and Collaboration Lab at the University of North Carolina at Chapel Hill is proud to support the digitization of the North Carolina Studies in the Romance Languages and Literatures series.

www.ingramcontent.com/pod-product-compliance
Lightning Source LLC
Chambersburg PA
CBHW030657230426
43665CB00011B/1131